BUILDING HIS FATHER'S BUSINESS

One Soul at a Time

The true story of a modern-day Apostle Paul
G.S. Nair, the Missionary-Entrepreneur of India

JACK MCELROY

McElroy Publishing
Transforming Hearts and Lives Since 1992

ISBN: 978-0-9860265-4-6 PB
ISBN: 978-0-9622191-7-7 Kindle
ISBN: 978-0-9622191-8-4 epub

McElroy Publishing
27-33 Fredonian Street
Shirley, MA 01464
978-425-4055
978-425-6116 Fax
info@mcelroypublishing.com

Interior book layout and design: Delaney-Designs, www.delaney-designs.com
Copyediting: Kathleen Deselle, Freelance Editing Services

<u>**India Contact**</u>

Dr. G.S. Nair, Director
P.O. Box 1216, Perurkada, P.O.
Trivandrum 695005 Kerala, India
011-91-471-2437352 Home
011-91-472-2899146 College Office
011-91-9447037352 Cell
gsnairpbm@gmail.com

Website: **http://www.gsnair.org**
Facebook: **https://www.facebook.com/PBMIndia?fref=ts**

<u>**United States Contact**</u>

Fundamental Baptist Mission to India
FBMI is a 501(c)(3) non-profit charitable organization

To support the ministry or to schedule Dr. Nair to speak at your church, please contact:

Mr. Don Chisholm
137 Scudder Rd.
Osterville, MA 02655
(508) 428-6989
dchisholm29@gmail.com

Checks should be made out and sent to:
Fundamental Baptist Mission to India
137 Scudder Rd.
Osterville, MA 02655

TABLE OF CONTENTS

PART 4
Ministry-building secrets of G.S. Nair revealed

PREFACE

And he said unto them, How is it that ye sought me?
*wist ye not that **I must be about my Father's business?***
(Luke 2:49)

I've always thought that anybody who is a successful church planter is really an entrepreneur. If they started a commercial business, I bet they would be successful at that too.

Folks in the church-planting business are in a people business, and they provide an extremely important service. They get people connected to the Lord Jesus Christ.

They continue to provide the service of ministering the word and prayer. They encourage believers to grow in grace and multiply themselves by witnessing for the Lord.

I've known G.S. Nair for about thirty-five years. The work that he does in India and the expansion of the ministry spanning nearly forty years has been phenomenal. As an entrepreneur, I can appreciate the qualities of entrepreneurship that G.S. has exhibited as the ministry has grown.

I recently saw a blog post titled "7 Ways Successful Entrepreneurs Think Differently."[1] It was written by a man named Jeet Banerjee, a young and successful entrepreneur from California.

Here is how I would apply this blogger's list to Dr. G.S. Nair.

1. **"They like having competitors."** I know, having competition sounds like a bad thing, doesn't it? But it really isn't. What it indicates is that there is a big market, and that means there are lots of people who

---

1   Jeet Banerjee, "7 Ways Successful Entrepreneurs Think Differently," posted September 23, 2014. Available online: http://www.jeetbanerjee.com/7-ways-successful-entrepreneurs-think-differently/ (accessed August 6, 2015).

need something; people with problems that need to be solved. Solving problems is what entrepreneurs get paid for.

When it comes to religious beliefs the market is huge, especially in India where there are about 1.5 billion people who do not know Jesus Christ. They are in the world, without hope and without God. And when they die they lose their own souls.

But we have a "product" that solves their monstrous problem. Our "product" is a personal relationship with the creator of all things—the Lord Jesus Christ. There is no better product. And there is no greater need than knowing him.

This is why G.S. has "ceased not to teach and preach Jesus" (Acts 5:42) with enthusiasm ever since he got saved in 1972.

2. **"They don't overlook any opportunity."** As Christians, our opportunities are finding ways to serve the Lord and others. G.S. has done that by creating ministries that are not only educational and humanitarian but evangelistic to boot.

3. **"They are perfectly fine with making mistakes."** We've all made them. I have. You have. And so has G.S. I call it "tuition." But what I really appreciate about G.S. is how he handles mistakes made by others—especially students and staff at the colleges and seminary operated by the ministry. He is always gracious and kind; firm but gentle. Even years afterward, people whom he's had to let go or students that have been dismissed still respect him.

4. **"They have vision."** When I consider more than 2,700 churches planted with new believers over the past thirty-nine years, *and* three Bible colleges, *and* a seminary, *and* fifteen extension schools, *and* seven

private Christian schools, *and* twenty orphanages—all started from scratch and flowing out of overnight prayer vigils in 1976—I am overwhelmed with his vision.

5. **"They can adapt quickly."** Every entrepreneur is familiar with Murphy's Law: Anything that can go wrong will go wrong. It's the one thing you can count on in business. But in the case of the ministry business it's more than that. God has an enemy. And that enemy is alive and well and seeking to stop the work of the ministry. G.S. experiences such resistance constantly, and as you'll discover as you read on, some of his experiences are up close and personal with the enemy.

6. **"They'd rather work more and earn less."** Entrepreneurs are always thinking about the future. Even if you're making no money now, you just know that your efforts are going to pay off down the road (you hope). We are willing to sacrifice now for the greater reward later.

The greater reward in the business of ministry is given out at the judgment seat of Christ. All the sacrifices made now will pay dividends then; although it's compensation enough to see so many come to know and love the Savior.

But right now, G.S. is focused on the cause and the work. The cause is the souls of men and women whose eternity is at stake; the work is reaching them with the gospel and encouraging them to reach others.

7. **"They don't look back."** Brother G.S. has no time to look back. There's too much work to be done, and he is always looking to the future—how he might reach more souls, how the ministry might provide for orphaned children, how they might reach more

lepers, how they might relieve suffering of disaster victims or victims of religious persecution.

I have always found G.S. to "press toward the mark for the prize of the high calling of God in Christ Jesus" (Philippians 3:14). As you read the following pages, I'm sure you will agree.

Jack McElroy
Groton, Massachusetts
September 2015

INTRODUCTION

This book will reveal the secret of how one man has planted more than 2,700 churches in four countries and has won more than 250,000 souls to Christ in thirty-nine years.

But it's how he'll be rewarded that could really affect you personally.

I know what you're thinking, Dear Reader.

It's impossible. One man can't do all that in thirty-nine years. And you're right, one man can't and didn't—acting alone. But…

An inspired leader can accomplish this and more.

But it's what this man could accomplish in the future that affects you. I'll get to that in a minute. But first let me introduce you to this extraordinary friend of mine who has accomplished so much for the Lord.

His name is Dr. G.S. Nair. He is a former Indian Army officer and high caste Hindu who was converted to the Lord Jesus Christ in 1972. And like the Apostle Paul after his conversion, the same can be said of Dr. Nair:

> *And straightway he preached Christ … that he is the Son of God. (Acts 9:20)*

I've known Brother G.S. since 1982. He has stayed in our home many times over the past thirty years. I've traveled with him to supporting churches in the United States. But more importantly, I have visited him and seen the ministry in India firsthand.

Here's what I take away from our relationship…

He reminds me of the Apostle Paul.

That may sound like a bold claim, but let me show you why I make it.

I can do it best by contrasting his appearance in the United States versus at home in India where he is "in the field."

First, when Brother G.S. visits supporting churches in the United States, he is usually introduced as "one of our missionaries." And so he is.

But missionaries just don't seem to have the "celebrity" status they once had. When they're at a new or supporting church, many folks just walk by with little thought or care about what missionaries are today and what they're doing. Perhaps this is because the cost of being a missionary today is low compared to what it was in the nineteenth and early twentieth centuries.

Modern transportation (cheap airline travel) and modern communications (Skype and email) have largely taken danger and daring out of the mix, and no one goes to the mission field to "die" anymore. So missionaries are sort of a commodity.

I've seen it in the way missionaries are treated when I've traveled with G.S. and I get it. Don't get me wrong. Brother G.S. is the last person to seek "celebrity status."

But it would be a shame to overlook this extraordinary man just as it would have been a shame to overlook the Apostle Paul when he came to town:

> *And when we were come to Jerusalem, the brethren received us gladly. (Acts 21:17)*

Second, Dr. Nair's thick Indian-English accent is sometimes hard to understand.

Like the Apostle Paul, G.S. is...

> ...*rude in speech, yet not in knowledge;*
> *(2 Corinthians 11:6)*

Yet this man of God speaks Malayalam (his native tongue), English, Hindi, and several Indian dialects. (I wonder what kind of accent the Apostle Paul had?)

Third, G.S. is not physically domineering and doesn't dress ostentatiously or try to "project an image" as being someone special.

> **DID YOU KNOW?**
>
> There are 1,800 dialects and over 100 languages spoken in India.

In fact, his demeanor is like that of the Apostle Paul, who said of himself,

> ...*who in presence am base among you, but being absent*
> *am bold toward you: (2 Corinthians 10:1)*

He is a humble and unassuming man. But here's what the average Christian doesn't see...

Back in India, the comparison is even more pronounced.

The Apostle Paul said,

> *Beside those things that are without, that which cometh*
> *upon me daily, the care of all the churches.*
> *(2 Corinthians 11:28)*

And, like Paul, G.S. travels extensively ministering to pastors and folks in the churches he's had a hand in planting.

Burdened for the welfare of the believers and edification of the saints, Brother G.S. constantly visits churches throughout India as well as the churches in three neighboring countries.

The Apostle Paul went on three missionary journeys that we're told of. I'm sure he would have gone on more if he'd had better transportation.

Brother G.S. has probably logged more miles than any three busy executives of multinational corporations.

DID YOU KNOW?

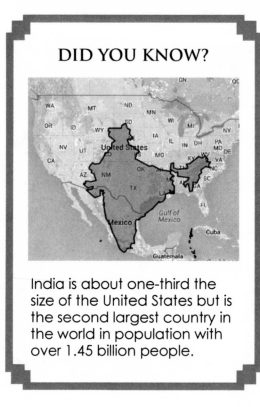

India is about one-third the size of the United States but is the second largest country in the world in population with over 1.45 billion people.

And then there are the church plants...

The Apostle Paul started many churches in his lifetime. And although G.S. has **personally** planted four churches to date, he's responsible for a couple of thousand more as you'll see.

I could go on comparing G.S. and the Apostle Paul, but I want to get to more important matters...

Who doesn't want to support church planters?

I've been in and around independent Baptist churches for over thirty-five years. Just about every church I know of wants to support church planters. In fact, most every pastor I know has a policy of only supporting missionaries who are church planters.

But G.S. has done more than that. He has multiplied himself by creating…

Eighteen "Church Planter" factories

I know it sounds weird, but because I'm a businessman that's what it looks like to me. The "factories" that G.S. has created include:

- 3 Bible Colleges
- 1 Seminary
- 15 Bible College Extension Schools

Through these facilities G.S. has trained more than 2,700 other church planters. The focus of the Bible colleges, Seminary, and Extension Schools is not just to graduate men who can pastor a church but men who can go out and start new churches—they are entrepreneurial pastors, if you will.

And isn't training men for the ministry what the Apostle Paul instructed Timothy to do?

> *And the things that thou hast heard of me among many witnesses, the same commit thou to faithful men, who shall be able to teach others also. (2 Timothy 2:2)*

What's important about these church planters is that they're nationals—folks from different parts of India and three neighboring countries who go back into their own states or countries to evangelize their kinsmen according to the flesh.

And why is that such a big deal?

Because unlike foreign missionaries, nationals don't have to go to language school[2] or adapt to a new culture. But of course even if you wanted to send foreign missionaries to India, you can't. India has been a closed mission field since 1978.

---

2   "How Long Does It Take to Learn a Language? Missionary Preparation Tip #19," YouTube video uploaded August 20, 2010. Available online: https://www.youtube.com/watch?v=-7VWQr-KvHc (accessed August 6, 2015).

And what church doesn't want its missionaries to be big-time soul winners?

Isn't that what we expect? Isn't that why we want "reports from the field" to assure us that the missions budget is being spent wisely?

> ## DID YOU KNOW?
>
> It takes the average missionary one to two years to learn another language proficiently and often longer to learn the nuances to be able to speak of spiritual matters.

Like the Apostle Paul, G.S. is a great evangelist. But he's more than that; he's a soul-winning leader who has developed a proven method of raising up and teaching others how to win souls by the thousands—to the tune of more than 250,000 souls won to Christ over the past thirty-nine years. That's right—250,000. Not 25, 250, or 2,500. Hey, even 25,000 would be considered phenomenal.

You've got to be wondering, how are these fellows taught the ropes?

The secret sauce is…

The world's most unusual summer job

Dr. Nair's Church Planting Summer Ministry Outreach is the grand engine of evangelism and the church planting model in India. They've used it for over thirty-nine years—because it works.

Instead of going home for summer break, many of the students and faculty members from the colleges serve with evangelistic teams, traveling throughout India to reach many for Christ. Typically, thirty or forty teams are sent out with about eleven students and one faculty member in each team.

Here's what each team does:

- Invite people to gospel meetings through door-to-door evangelism.
- Hand out hundreds of thousands of tracts each summer.
- Hold open-air meetings, Bible studies, and cottage meetings.
- Preach, sing, and give testimonies at evangelistic meetings.
- Deal one-on-one with inquirers, seeking to lead them to Christ.
- Do follow-up work that results in Bible studies, baptism of new converts, and establishing new churches.

The Results

Through these efforts, more than 2,700 churches have been founded in all twenty-nine states of India and in neighboring countries such as Nepal, Myanmar, and Bhutan.

These churches are composed of more than 250,000 souls.

Over 100 home Bible studies are being conducted in preparation for becoming newly organized local assemblies. Plans are also being made to enter Bangladesh, Sri Lanka, Pakistan, and other countries.

Over the past thirty-nine years, the Lord has blessed the "church planter" ministries with over 2,700 graduates—with many more helping in various ministries (children's home, Christian schools, etc.). Over 80 percent of these graduates go on to full-time service for the Lord. That's an astounding rate of faithfulness among the graduates of the colleges.

But here's the amazing thing; in addition to all his responsibilities...

G.S. Nair is still a local church pastor.

G.S. always tells folks in his presentation in the United States that he is a pastor. And that he is. In 1978 he founded and is still pastor of Peoples Baptist Church in Trivandrum, Kerala State, India. Even with his great responsibilities and travels, Dr. Nair is still a local church pastor with a pastor's heart.

DID YOU KNOW?

Until Baptist missionary William Carey (1761–1834) fought for change, when a husband died, his widow was thrown onto his funeral pyre and his children were offered to idols. Today, widows and children are often considered outcasts and destined to live in extreme poverty.

Not only is Pastor G.S. committed to the ministry of the Word, but like our Savior, G.S. is a compassionate man having pity on the fatherless and widows...

Pure religion and undefiled before God and the Father is this, To visit the fatherless and widows in their affliction, and to keep himself unspotted from the world.

(James 1:27)

His compassion and leadership has produced...

20 children's homes...

Some call them orphanages. But he doesn't.

That's because the children are cared for by a pastor, his wife, and members of local churches. They don't see the children as "orphaned" anymore. They are members of a family. And lots of these kids come to know the Lord Jesus Christ as their own Savior.

Can you imagine how much that means to each of the 494 little ones they care for? By the way, the ministry doesn't go looking for orphans. There are plenty of them. But G.S. has a special and unique way of developing these homes to ensure that they remain both nurturing and evangelistic.

...and many additional ministries

I could go on about how the mission also operates seven private Christian schools in six states with an enrollment of 850 students for the purpose of providing quality education, teaching Christian doctrine, and evangelizing youth.

Plus there's the two vocational training centers for women, an assisted living home, a ministry to lepers in two Indian states (yes, there is still leprosy in India), two ladies' homes (providing for eleven women, mostly widows, some of whom have been rejected by their families because of their faith in Christ), and a home for thirty abused girls. Plus, a New Drug Rehabilitation Center and medical ministry are in the works.

If you ever get the chance to spend time with him, don't miss the opportunity to experience...

A true visionary

Sometimes all we see is the speaker behind the pulpit with a PowerPoint presentation, but brother G.S. is so much more than that. He is a Spirit-filled visionary who has set up an evangelistic and charitable ministry that actually does everything we say we believe in.

So if you ever get the opportunity to meet and speak to this extraordinary man, grab it.

Spend as much time as you can with him and let his vision challenge and warm your heart. You won't find many other men today who will inspire you like Brother Nair.

But as I mentioned earlier...

It's how he'll be rewarded that really affects you personally.

Here's what I mean. We've all been taught about rewards and crowns the Lord will give to faithful servants, and no doubt G.S. is in line for his. But others will be standing alongside him and getting rewards for his deeds as well. Here's a special story and how you can be included in this group...

None of Dr. Nair's accomplishments ever would've happened had it not been for a medical missionary and three or four elderly widows.

In 1971, G.S. was diagnosed with tuberculosis and admitted to a Baptist Mid-Missions hospital. While there he came to know the Lord Jesus as his Savior through reading the Bible and the persistent witness of a medical missionary doctor named Quentin Kenoyer and his nurse-wife, Marleah. They served the Lord faithfully in India for twenty-six years. It's been said of Dr. Kenoyer that "Today, some of the influential pastors in the area testify that they heard the gospel of Jesus Christ while they were patients" at his hospital.[3]

But here's the thing; contributions to that hospital ministry were made by...

Three or four elderly widows

Here are the details of their more than hundredfold return on investment.

Although many people helped to build Burrows Memorial Christian Hospital, here's a story G.S. relates about the tuberculosis (TB) sanatorium from missionaries who work there.

---

3   "Quentin Kenoyer, Medical Missionary," General Association of Regular Baptist Churches. Available online: http://www.garbc.org/news/quentin-kenoyer-retired-medical-missionary/ (accessed August 17, 2015).

They told him that three or four widows financed the building of the TB sanatorium and especially the ward in which he was kept. These ladies never knew how the Lord would eventually multiply their investment by the hundreds of thousands of saved souls that would be credited to their account.

Like the Scripture says, "Cast thy bread upon the waters: for thou shalt find it after many days" (Ecclesiastes 11:1).

On the Day of Judgment there will be several widow ladies who will receive great rewards because it was their sacrificial giving that helped one medical missionary reach one man through whom the Lord has already reached more than 250,000 souls.

How's that for more than a hundredfold return on investment?

They gave because there was a cause—the souls of men and women for whom the Lord Jesus Christ died. G.S. Nair works because of this cause.

Those ladies sacrificially gave to a work that they prayed would win some people to the Lord Jesus Christ.

But they had no idea how their prayers would be answered. They could never have anticipated the return on their investment. What they didn't know was that one of the folks who would be won to the Lord would be a high caste Hindu Indian Army officer named G.S. Nair who, like the Apostle Paul, would be

> *...a chosen vessel unto me, to bear my name before the Gentiles... (Acts 9:15)*

And they never would have dreamed that through G.S. Nair and his ministry, more than 250,000 people would come to know the Lord Jesus Christ as their own Savior—that's a lot of fruit from their prayers and sacrificial giving.

We all know from Scripture that there's a judgment day coming when the Lord is going to hand out crowns.

I can see the tears of joy flowing down their faces as the Lord rewards these widow ladies abundantly above all they could've ever asked or thought. He's already told each of them, "Well done, thou good and faithful servant."

They've already heard those words. But this will be another time when all can rejoice at the work the Lord has done in them and through them.

Does the Lord care about what those widows did? You bet he does. Consider the widow's mite. Although we don't know her name, we do know her deed. But someday we will know her name. And someday we will know the names of those ladies as well.

I'm happy for them now, but I'll be rejoicing "with exceeding great joy" then.

But what about you?

You can't go on the streets of India teeming with lost souls and hand out tracts. You can't preach to or teach these folks who desperately need to know the truth. Even if you wanted to, you can't. You can't get a missionary visa to do any of these things in the country of India.

But you can change the world in a big way—one soul at a time—by investing in a whole army of men and women who are ready to do these things in your stead.

You can become that foreign missionary to India by investing in them just like those ladies invested in the hospital that was instrumental in the salvation of G.S. Nair.

You are not just investing in "a missionary," but in a life-changing, dynamic, international ministry that is comprehensive (everything we say we believe in—they do); built on a biblical model (the ministry of a local church); and seasoned with thirty-nine years of efficient, cost-effective, and extraordinary results.

Building his Father's business

I invite you to learn more about this extraordinary modern-day Apostle Paul in the following pages. You will read in Brother Nair's own words the story of his conversion and call to ministry. You will get a glimpse of his remarkable prayer life and witness the trials as well as triumphs as he continues to be about his Father's business.

Postscript

Although he was hostile to the gospel, G.S. never "made havoc of the church" (Acts 7:3) as did the unconverted Saul.

The parallels to the Apostle Paul are in his travels, teaching, preaching, soul winning, church planting, discipleship, edification of the saints, and work of the ministry as you will soon find out.

PART 1

High caste Hindu trades 330 million gods for one—
The salvation and development of
the missionary-entrepreneur of India

CHAPTER 1

Hindu high caste Army man gets tuberculosis

Jesus sought me when a stranger,
Wandering from the fold of God;
He, to rescue me from danger,
Interposed His precious blood.[4]

G.S. Nair was born December 23, 1949, into the Nair family. They are Brahmans—the highest ranking of the four social classes in Hindu India. His parents "did the right thing" when they dedicated him unto their Hindu gods. He was named Govindan Sreedharan (G.S.) after the Hindu god Krishna.

He grew up as a religious Hindu and followed the rituals prescribed by his religion. But there was a problem...

But nothing satisfied me, a deep emptiness began to grow. A deep, deep emptiness began to grow in the worst manner. I was so helpless and dissatisfied—without peace and joy. I began to think that if I just got a job that would take my emptiness away.

G.S. Nair as a young boy

---

4   Robert Robinson, "Come Thou Fount of Every Blessing" (1757). Robinson wrote this Christian hymn at age 22. Available online: https://en.wikipedia.org/wiki/Come_Thou_Fount_of_Every_Blessing

His stepfather was cruel and unmerciful. So in order to escape the unkindness at home and to change his life, eighteen-year-old Govindan Nair joined the Indian Army in 1967.

G.S. was very ambitious and worked hard. He became an officer. Even while in the army he continued his ritualistic prayers and actions. In 1970 he was transferred to the northeastern part of India on the border of what is now known as Bangladesh and Myanmar (Burma). It was there that he contracted tuberculosis (TB).

The disease was killing him. Providentially, his superiors discovered a hospital run by doctors from Baptist Mid-Missions where there was a tuberculosis sanatorium.

The army sent him to Burrows Memorial Christian Hospital for treatment. It was there that he first heard the gospel of the Lord Jesus Christ. He was anything but receptive.

Missionary doc meets a tough case

In sports as well as in real life, you want to make sure that you "leave it all on the field." Such was the case of Dr. Quentin Kenoyer (1924–2014) and his wife, Marleah. They were in charge of the hospital. And if you've ever read any books about missionary heroes, these two folks qualify.[5] For twenty-six years they served the Lord faithfully in India. Dr. Kenoyer was the son of a builder and she a farmer's daughter.

Dr. Quentin Kenoyer, a faithful servant of the Lord

5   You'll be inspired by a short (less than ten minutes) video produced by Baptist Mid-Missions about the Kenoyers: "Quentin and Marleah Kenoyer," Baptist Mid-Missions video. Available online: https://www.facebook.com/BaptistMidMissions/videos/870312116 321975/?pnref=story

According to Baptist Mid-Missions[6]:

> Although Quentin's passion had always been medicine, he
> was no less passionate about bearing testimony to the love
> of Christ and boldly sharing the gospel with any and all who
> entered his circle ... Each Sunday he would preach during a
> chapel for the patients at the hospital, attend church himself,
> then go into the community with a team to evangelize.
>
> His willingness to serve patients, his skill as a doctor, and his
> kindness brought many people to the hospital.

And more importantly,

> Today, some of the influential pastors in the area testify that
> they heard the gospel of Jesus Christ while they were patients
> at his hospital.
>
> Literally hundreds of thousands of people have come to
> know the Lord through the men and women that were saved
> under the Kenoyers' ministry.

G.S. Nair was one of them.

Dr. Kenoyer came to Burrows Memorial in 1951 and over the years
turned it into a state-of-the-art hospital. He and his family labored
there until they were forced to leave in 1977.

In addition to working as a nurse, Mrs. Kenoyer founded the
Burrows Memorial Christian Hospital School of Nursing in India
and became its first director.[7] The school recently celebrated its fifty-
fourth graduation ceremony. Even today, nursing students study the
Bible via correspondence courses, attend Sunday School classes

---

6   "Quentin Kenoyer, Medical Missionary," General Association of Regular Baptist
Churches, December 18, 2014. Available online: http://www.garbc.org/news/quentin-
kenoyer-retired-medical-missionary/ (accessed August 20, 2015).

7   "Marleah Kenoyer, Medical Missionary," General Association of Regular Baptist
Churches, July 23, 2015. Available online: http://www.garbc.org/news/marleah-kenoyer-
medical-missionary/ (accessed September 2, 2015).

and a student fellowship, and participate in morning devotions with singing and prayer for the hospital patients.[8]

Burrows Memorial Christian Hospital

I'm looking forward to the day I'll get to meet the Kenoyers.[9]

G.S. ended up being parked in the sanatorium for eighteen months. It was here that he ran into this sold-out-to-the-Lord missionary doctor, his nurse-wife, and a staff of like-minded, committed missionaries.

---

8   Emmanuel Hospital Association, "Burrows Memorial Christian Hospital." Available online: http://www.ehausa.org/hospitals_burrows_memorial_christian.html (accessed September 2, 2015).

9   Although there are many people that helped to build the hospital, G.S. relates a story about the TB sanatorium told by missionaries who work there: Three or four widows financed the building of the TB sanatorium and especially the ward in which he stayed as a patient. These ladies never knew how the Lord would eventually multiply their investment by the hundreds of thousands of saved souls that would be credited to their account.

Like the Scripture says, "Cast thy bread upon the waters: for thou shalt find it after many days" (Ecclesiastes 11:1). On the Day of Judgment there will be several widow ladies who will receive great rewards because it was through their sacrificial giving that one medical missionary reached one man through whom the Lord has already reached more than 250,000 souls.

I entered the hospital in 1971. As they went along with my treatment, this missionary doctor began to share the love of Jesus Christ with me. Being a Hindu believing in 330 million gods and goddesses, why should I believe in this western God? That was my question to this doctor. Anyway, he did not argue with me, he began to share the love of Jesus Christ with me.

G.S. attended the Bible studies because, like he says:

As a patient you always have to please the doctor.

At one of the Bible studies, I heard him [Dr. Kenoyer] preach that without Jesus there is no way possibly for any man or woman to be saved. I was extremely angry at the doctor for saying this.

Why should he accept some foreign God? He already had plenty of gods. And who needed a God that claimed exclusivity for the position? The only God? It couldn't be so.

I'd argue with them like mad. But this man was very kind, giving; and he knew that the god of this world had blinded my eyes. They needed to be opened to the gospel of the Lord Jesus Christ. So he continually prayed and gave the gospel to me without getting angry with me.

G.S. was well-known in the hospital as having a bitter and argumentative spirit. Although not a militant Hindu, he was a "good" Hindu—someone who believed in his faith and wasn't timid about defending it, someone who knew enough to put up his guard against foreign devils who deny that his faith and his god isn't sufficient.

Not to be outdone, G.S. got hold of a Bible and began to read so that he could argue his point.

Now that shows what type of man he is at the core. He actually read the Bible to dispute Christianity. He didn't give off-the-cuff answers or insincere arguments. He did his homework. He did his research.

This is another sign of a true entrepreneur—you study competing products so you can effectively compete.

But what G.S. didn't know was that the product he was competing against was a personal relationship with the sole God and creator of all things. Plus, the competing sales rep for the Lord's side was none other than the Holy Ghost himself. And worse, G.S. was competing against the Word of God, which is quick and powerful and sharper than a two-edged sword.

While seeking to disprove Christianity, he was seeking to disprove the words of the living God who will not be disproved.

If any man is a sincere seeker (like Nicodemus), he will find God. And G.S. was sincere. He just didn't realize how deficient his religious product was.

Through the Bible in six months

> I began to read the Bible so I could argue with these people, showing that my religion, my karma, my ritualism, our kind of devotion is much greater than that of these people. With that in mind, I started reading the Word of God. I didn't know it was the Word of God at the time, but I started reading it and taking it out of context. I began to argue with the people, those who come across my bed.
>
> Arguing became a habit for me. I argued with these missionaries for months, but I kept on reading the Word of God. I read through the Bible completely within six months.
>
> And I continued to argue with these people. At around seven or eight months' time I began to notice that the same people who used to come near my bed to pray with and talk to me started to avoid me because I was wasting their time.

The patience of a saint (literally)

> But Dr. Kenoyer never gave me up. Whenever he came, he would share the gospel of the Lord Jesus Christ with me. I tried to provoke him, make him angry with arguments or other kinds of problems, but he never got mad at me. He knew that the god of this world had blinded my eyes, and they could only be opened through the gospel of the Lord Jesus Christ.

Dr. Kenoyer never quit. He never argued because, like G.S. says:

> You don't win someone to the Lord by arguing.

And Dr. Kenoyer understood what the Scripture says:

> *And the servant of the Lord must not strive; but be gentle unto all men, apt to teach, patient, In meekness instructing those that oppose themselves; if God peradventure will give them repentance to the acknowledging of the truth; And that they may recover themselves out of the snare of the devil, who are taken captive by him at his will. (2 Timothy 2:24-26)*

As time went on, G.S. continued to read the Word of God, but his health deteriorated despite being injected with more than 400 shots of Streptomycin. None of the shots did any good, but rather the high dosage of antibiotics made him sicker.

> I saw people literally die with TB in that hospital; some of them were my friends. I was frustrated, disappointed, and full of anxiety. So I decided to pray to Jesus along with my other gods and goddesses. But that didn't bring anything good because Jesus Christ is not one of the gods, he's the only God, he's the living God.

Third time's a charm

G.S. continued to read God's Word, and by the time eighteen months had passed he had read through the Bible completely two times and was beginning his third go-round. Sadly, many Christians haven't read the Bible through once in a lifetime.

> The problem with me was that I did not want to admit I was a lost sinner and that I needed a living savior.

> Many religions of this world teach that it is sin to say that man is a sinner. I have read that kind of philosophy many times, and yet the Bible says: "For all have sinned, and come short of the glory of God."[10]

The sinner was about to meet his match...

---

10   Romans 3:23

CHAPTER 2

His conversion, healing, and call to His ministry

How firm a foundation, ye saints of the Lord,
Is laid for your faith in His excellent word!
What more can He say than to you He hath said,
To you who for refuge to Jesus have fled?[11]

The sword of the Spirit does its job

I am a sinner, but it was difficult for me to realize that. After eighteen months while I was reading the Bible for the third time, I came across Jeremiah 17:9. The Word of God says: "The heart is deceitful above all things, and desperately wicked: who can know it?"

That was the first time in my life that God's spirit began to convict me of my sin. He made me realize that my heart was so blackened with sin that it could only be opened by God himself.

With the burden and the guilt of my sin, I started crying in my bed. At the same time, I began to look back to our religious beliefs. The Bhagavad Gita [a 700-verse Hindu scripture] says "god often comes to destroy the wicked and save the righteous."

---

11   John Rippon, "How Firm a Foundation" (1787), in *A Selection of Hymns from the Best Authors, Intended to be an Appendix to Dr. Watts' Psalms and Hymns.* In what is known as "Rippon's Selection," this Christian hymn "is attributed only to 'K,' which probably refers to Robert Keen(e), precentor at Rippon's church, though other names suggested include Richard or John Keene, Kirkham, or John Keith." Available online: https://en.wikipedia.org/wiki/How_Firm_a_Foundation_%28hymn%29

But truly the Bible says, "There is none righteous, no, not one" and "For all have sinned, and come short of the glory of God," which means I am a lost sinner without a hope in any religion.[12]

Jesus Christ came to this world to seek and to save that which was lost. By him going to the cross of Calvary for my sin, he paid the penalty of my sin; by giving his body on the cross of Calvary—by shedding his blood—he died for me. Like the scripture says:

... *without shedding of blood is no remission. (Hebrews 9:22)*

Thank God he not only died and was buried; he's risen from the dead!

The Bible says if any man or woman will call upon the name of the Lord, they shall be saved. I heard the gospel hundreds of times; I read the Bible and all this brought me to Jesus Christ, the living and only Savior, who gave his life for my sin.

He's able to save me. I called out to him that morning and asked him to come into my heart.

And what about you, dear friend? Have you invited Jesus into your heart?

I strongly believe that if any man or woman calls on the name of the Lord, they shall be saved.

The Lord Jesus Christ heard my prayer; he came into my heart, forgave my sin, and made me a child of God. The guilt was removed and the burden of sin was rolled away; instead of emptiness I was filled with joy and happiness.

---

12   Romans 3:10 and Romans 3:23

Now life became worth living. I am a child of God.

Christianity is the only religion that makes a sinner become a child of God. All others simply make one religious.

G.S. and his wife, Sarah, in 2012. Forty years earlier, he had accepted the Lord at this hospital after being witnessed to for eighteen months by hospital staff.

New operating system installed

Salvation is like the installation of a new operating system in your computer—except it's got no bugs in it and it actually works the way it's supposed to. (Christianity changes sinners from the inside out. The religions of this world may change the outside but never get inside.)

We all get a new heart installed, but it manifests itself in different ways for each of us. (That's one of the reasons why it's so neat to hear people's testimonies.)

For example, the Apostle Paul was **shut down** for three days after the initial install. Paul asked the Lord, "What will thou have me to do?" The only answer he got "was three days without sight" (Acts 9:6, 9).

After three days, scales fell off his eyes and the Lord **powered him up** again with the new operating system.

G.S. was "filled with the Holy Ghost" (Acts 9:17) and his new heart was evidenced by tears and shouting (or at least the desire to do so).

> Yes, I am a child of God. Everything became new! I wanted to shout "Hallelujah!" but it's a hospital.
>
> I went down and met with Dr. Kenoyer and prayed. I came back to my room, but I couldn't go back to my bed.

Little did Dr. Kenoyer know that G.S. was "a chosen vessel" whom the Lord would use "to bear my name before" tens of thousands of people in India and lands beyond.

His new Christian heart and character now began to manifest his fervency and love for the Lord Jesus Christ...

And like the Apostle Paul after his conversion...

> *And straightway he preached Christ... (Acts 9:20)*

> I began to think of how I misled many people in this hospital, so I began to go around talking to people sharing the gospel of the Lord Jesus Christ. It was an astonishing surprise for many people. But some ridiculed and hated me because I changed my religion.

That reminds me of what they said about Paul...

> *But all that heard him were amazed... (Acts 9:21)*

> Until that previous day I was arguing against Christianity, trying to tell people our religion is better than any other religion and that these foreigners are making this up.

> But God began to work in my heart—a good work.
> He made me to realize that he forgave my sin and
> now I am a child of God. I had the joy and peace
> that passes all understanding.

As fervently against Christ as he was before, like Paul, he became
fervently for Christ. And he finally found the peace that had eluded
him as a younger man.

> I couldn't be silent but began to share the gospel
> of the Lord Jesus Christ; although that caused a
> problem because people with TB should not be
> talking so much.

The Lord heals G.S.

> So they put me on bed rest. And then we prayed.
> And God in his mighty mercy not only saved me, he
> healed me from tuberculosis. Within two months
> I was able to get out of the hospital after an x-ray.
> The doctor couldn't believe I was completely free
> from TB!

> Before I left, I obeyed the Lord by being baptized at
> Alipur Baptist Church on the mission compound. I
> was baptized by Pastor Ajit Paul, a converted Hindu
> who was also a tuberculosis patient. Pastor Paul
> was an instrument used by God to share the gospel,
> and he began to show me more Scriptures on how
> to obey the Lord. Soon thereafter, I left the hospital
> and went back to the army.

G.S. was baptized at Alipur Baptist Church soon after being saved.

Pastor Ajit Paul, on the left, baptized G.S.

And he would go on to make history in the land of India as we will see shortly…

But first, things went bad on the home front when his parents found out he had rejected their religion and embraced a foreign cult.

Meanwhile, my parents got upset with me. Being a high caste Hindu whose life was dedicated to some of the Hindu gods and goddesses, they knew I had rejected their religious beliefs and practices, which they had taught me since I was a child. They felt like I had put their religion down into the mud.

The Lord turned me away from the falsity of their religion. I changed my beliefs. So they began to talk to me about whether my salvation and commitment to the Lord Jesus Christ was true.

But I had peace, happiness, joy, and even the hope he has given to me in the Lord. I could not go back from that.

His new heart had a tremendous burden for souls

They ostracized me from the family, but I could not hate them. I began to pray for their souls because they gave their best to my life. Without Jesus, I know God's Word says anyone will die and be eternally lost. So I was always conscious to maintain a bridge between us.

I thought about my grandmother who died in 1967 when she was eighty-eight years old. She was one of the best women I ever knew. But to the best of my knowledge she never heard the gospel of the Lord Jesus Christ. And according to the Bible, she's lost.

The thought of more of my people being lost was overwhelming. They need to hear this gospel of hope.

That's the very reason the Lord Jesus Christ came to this world. If there was any other way men could get saved from their sins, Jesus would not have come and died on the cross of Calvary.

The call to the ministry

I knew that God was calling me to the ministry, and I knew that everyone—those who don't have the gospel—are going to eternal damnation. That brought me really a kind of aggressiveness and compassion to just tell the gospel to other people.

But I knew I needed some basic knowledge. I was just a baby in the Lord Jesus Christ, so I said "I need go to Bible College."

Hunger for the Word

G.S. has read the Bible through many times in English as well as his native language. How else could such a profound ministry be started except for such a firm foundation? And what a firm foundation the Lord has laid for us in his excellent word ... and what a refuge he is for lost souls that flee to him.

> I was longing for the Word of God. I strongly believe that's one of the great signs of people who have gotten saved. There has to be a longing, a desire for God's Word.

One of the things that has surprised G.S. over the years is how that people sometimes say they have gotten saved but they just don't have any longing for God's word.

> I really just started with that because I was a baby, and although I had life, I needed food. God's Word is our food.

The Lord's hand in G.S.' discharge from the army

He went back to active service in the army but had no more interest in it. Even during the time that he was on active duty he used to hand out tracts.

He wanted to get out of the army but that wasn't going to be easy. Although the military had not paid him any salary while he was sick, they did pay for his eighteen-month hospital stay, so why should they let him go?

So he did what has become the hallmark of his ministry ... he prayed.

> So I prayed continually for six months. I finally told my commanding officer that God has worked in my heart; I found the Lord Jesus Christ, I know God's mercy, and I want to serve him.

> God worked in his heart and without any resistance he accepted my resignation and so I was released from the army. This was a tremendous answer to prayer since the military had paid for my recovery at the TB hospital.

Once he was discharged from the army, he went back to the hospital to see Dr. Kenoyer.

> He suggested that I go to Berean Baptist Bible College located in Bangalore. But he asked, "How are you going to support yourself?" I said, "I will trust the Lord." Oh, really? But I was really trusting what I had in my hand. Sometimes people can talk big because they have something in their hands.

> I had enough money that I had saved from my pay as an army officer. Plus I had my clothes, so I said "I'm going to make it." Those days, and even now, if I have little bit I'll do it.

So the young convert headed off to Bible College with the self-confidence and assurance of all budding entrepreneurs. That confidence would soon be shaken by ... who else but our Lord and Savior, Jesus Christ?

> Oftentimes the Lord uses the school of hard knocks to get the attention of his beloved followers so that he can guide them into trusting him as their Father. The trials form the foundation of the close relationship between the believer and our Father in heaven.

That's what's coming up next, and like it says in the Patch the Pirate song, *Rejoice in the Lord...*

CHAPTER 3

Tried, purified, molded, and trained by the Lord

God never moves without purpose or plan
When trying His servant and molding a man....
O rejoice in the Lord, He makes no mistake.
He knoweth the end of each path that I take.
For when I am tried and purified,
I shall come forth as gold.[13]

Trial number 1: Robbed!

So I took the train from Assam to Calcutta and then on to Bangalore. And I was robbed. I lost my army bags and all my money. I was left with my sandals, the clothes I was wearing, 35 rupees (which in today's money is not even one dollar), and my New Testament.

The train came to the station in Madras. I got down and I was so panicked I didn't know what to do. So I just sat and cried. What shall I do? Where shall I go? If I go back home my parents will say, "Where is your God?" I don't want somebody challenging me and putting my God down. I sat; then I prayed for a few hours. Then I took out my New Testament and I read my life verse:

Faithful is he that calleth you, who also will do it.
(1 Thessalonians 5:24)

---

13   Ron Hamilton ("Patch the Pirate"), Copyright 1980 in "Choral Arrangements Everybody Can Sing," Vol. 6, by Musical Ministries. Available online: http://ifcamedia.org/ifcaweb/pubs/ifcachera/CHERASPRING03.pdf

> Then I said, "Lord, if you're faithful I'm going to go."
> So I went to Bangalore with what I had; just what
> I was wearing, 35 rupees, and the New Testament.
> But God really began to teach me how to depend
> upon him—on a daily basis.

The Lord used the robbery to get G.S. to trust in him alone. But that was just the start of a lifetime where the Lord has constantly challenged G.S. to trust in him alone.

Trial number 2: Learning to depend on the Lord for daily needs

So the twenty-four-year-old newly minted born-again Christian entered Berean Baptist Bible College in Bangalore, India. Little did he know but that years later he would serve on the board of directors of his alma mater.

While there he learned to trust the Lord for small things; from a daily cup of tea to a shaving blade. Which the Lord was faithful to supply.

> I needed to have a cup of tea every day. It was a
> habit I developed in the army. Even though it seems
> like a small thing, I depended upon the Lord even
> for the few pennies I needed just to get some tea,
> and God provided faithfully.
>
> Even for a blade for shaving, he provided for me.
> Sometimes I would pray and God would work in
> other people's hearts. I don't even remember how
> many people helped me. When I opened my Bible,
> there were some rupees. When I moved my pillows,
> there was some money left there, envelopes of it. The
> Lord met all of my needs during the eighteen months
> in the hospital, and now he started to meet my needs
> at the college.
>
> But I did not know that he was building me up for a
> greater ministry.

That reminds me of what the Apostle Paul said we're supposed to be:

Rejoicing in hope; patient in tribulation; continuing instant in prayer. (Romans 12:12)

The foundation of the ministry is the Lord's faithfulness in answering prayer.

As G.S. says:

> I strongly believe and teach that any difficulty that God sends your way is God working in your life to build you up for a greater ministry. He is working in your life so that you will trust him more and more. If I was not able to trust him for a cup of tea and a blade for shaving and a shirt or any of my clothes, how am I going to trust him to provide for over 2,500 pastors today?
>
> So the lesson I learned was that every trouble will lead you to a greater future as you trust in God.

One of my favorite hymns is "I serve a risen Savior." And I do! He really does walk with me and talk with me along life's narrow way.

And verse one says:

> *I know that He is living,*
> *Whatever men may say.*
> *I see His hand of mercy;*
> *I hear His voice of cheer;*
> *And just the time I need Him*
> *He's always near.*[14]

Learning the ropes in the Christian service business

Every entrepreneur has to start somewhere, and usually that somewhere is working for somebody else. That's how you learn the ropes. It's how you get product knowledge and experience. And it was no different for this missionary-entrepreneur. The story continues…

> As I was studying at Berean Bible College in Bangalore, it really got driven into my heart to preach the gospel. The first thing that challenged me came in 1973, when **Every Home Crusade** visited the college seeking to assemble a team of approximately fifty to seventy people to go and evangelize in the desert area of Rajasthan in the northwest portion of India bordered by Pakistan.

Every Home Crusade, now known as Every Home for Christ International[15] was started in 1946. This group is dedicated to the Great Commission—to reach all people in every nation with the gospel and to disciple them in the Lord's ways. They first came to India in 1964.

---

14   Alfred H. Ackley, "He Lives" (1933). This hymn is more popularly known by Christians everywhere by its first line, "I serve a risen Savior."

15   Every Home for Christ, http://www.ehc.org/ (accessed August 20, 2015).

G.S. was an excited volunteer. As the Lord would have it, his leadership capabilities presented themselves and he was appointed to be leader of the group.

"Somehow" they knew.

> I was appointed leader of this group. Somehow even they knew that I was really concerned for souls. They made us organize a prayer meeting during that trip to Rajasthan. But because of the struggles, because the heat is so much, nearly 120°F, around 80 to 90 percent of the people went back.
>
> And within a month, we thinned to myself and two others. I stuck with it. We traveled, many times by bicycle. I fell unconscious a couple of times because of the extreme heat. We also faced financial struggles. Finally, the other two men became sick as well. We could not go on, and it was time to go back to college anyway.
>
> But we conducted soul-winning meetings by trusting the Lord. It motivated me to pray for our daily needs. What is important is that my "summer ministry evangelism" model came from this experience.

The Rajasthan experience was intended by the Lord so that G.S. would trust in him alone on the field. And over the next forty years, that daily trusting was necessary through the threats, persecutions, trials, and burdens (financial and otherwise) that would come his way. Not to mention the care for the churches and the concern for the pastors and the love that he has toward the children in the orphanages—all the folks who are ministered to through the ministries of Peoples Baptist Church. We all have burdens; he just as more than most because of the expanse of the ministry.

I've heard him speak many times of trusting and praying. Praying to G.S. is like breathing. His training in prayer is coming up next...

CHAPTER 4

Prevailing prayer—answers and strengthening from his heavenly Father

For every one that asketh receiveth; and he that seeketh findeth; and to him that knocketh it shall be opened. If a son shall ask bread of any of you that is a father, will he give him a stone? or if he ask a fish, will he for a fish give him a serpent? (Luke 11:10-11)

Isn't it interesting how the Lord sometimes uses young "all-in" committed college students and then does great things with them?

That was the case a little over two hundred years ago when five students started what became known as the Haystack Prayer Meeting at Williams College in Williamstown, Massachusetts, in August 1806.

Many scholars view this prayer event as the origin of Protestant missions in the United States.

A plaque on the campus of Williams College memorializes the Haystack Prayer Meeting, which sparked the American Foreign Mission movement.

Here's a quick overview...

Five Williams College students met in the summer of 1806, in a grove of trees near the Hoosic River, in what was then known as Sloan's Meadow, and debated the theology of missionary service. Their meeting was interrupted by a thunderstorm and the students: Samuel John Mills, James Richards, Robert C. Robbins, Harvey Loomis, and Byram Green, took shelter under a haystack until the sky cleared. "The brevity of the shower, the strangeness of the place of refuge, and the peculiarity of their topic of prayer and conference all took hold of their imaginations and their memories."

In 1808 the Haystack Prayer group and other Williams students began a group called "The Brethren." This group was organized to "effect, in the persons of its members, a mission to" those who were not Christians. In 1812, the American Board of Commissioners for Foreign Missions (created in 1810) sent its first missionaries to the non-Christian world, to India.

During the 19th century, it sent missionaries to China, Hawaii, and other nations in southeast Asia, establishing hospitals and schools at its mission stations. Many of its missionaries undertook translation of the Bible into native languages, and some created written languages where none had existed before. Thousands of missioners were sent to Asia, and they taught numerous indigenous peoples.

Samuel John Mills was most influential among the Haystack group to direct the modern mission movement. He played a role in the founding of the American Bible Society and the United Foreign Missionary Society.[16]

---

16   "Haystack Prayer Meeting," Wikipedia, last modified August 5, 2015. Available online: http://en.wikipedia.org/wiki/Haystack_Prayer_Meeting

Interestingly, Luther Rice (1783–1836) also became part of "the Brethren" at Williams College. Although not at the famous "Haystack prayer meeting," Rice became one of the group's leaders and in 1812 sailed to Calcutta, India, with Adoniram Judson. There he met William Carey, already in India.

While he did not remain in India, Rice did spend the rest of his career in the United States promoting missions, raising funds, and pushing for a united Baptist missionary-sending body. His work eventually led to the establishment of the Southern Baptist convention.[17]

What is interesting is that the focus early on for these missionaries was the country of India.

Now fast-forward about two hundred years…

The 1974 Indian "Haystack" prayer meeting

G.S. tells the story:

> In the spring of 1974, when I came back to the college, I really wanted to do outreach work so we formed a prayer group among the students. We started with around seven people. After that, others joined and we had around twenty-five to thirty students every Saturday and spent about half the night in prayer.

Who could've known then how the Lord would answer those prayers? One thing is certain; the Lord saw the commitment of that twenty-five-year-old college student and decided to use him in a great way. It was at that time they came up with a plan for that coming summer. This went on every summer until graduation three years later.

---

17   "Luther Rice," Wikipedia, last modified April 28, 2015. Available online: http://en.wikipedia.org/wiki/Luther_Rice

Four guys, five bucks, and the leadership of the Holy Spirit

Upon graduation along with three college friends, five dollars, and the guidance of the Holy Spirit, G.S. ventured out to hold open-air meetings, give testimonies, hand out tracts, and conduct Bible studies.

The burden of seeing millions going to hell combined with the compassion of our Savior motivated them to forsake all and give their lives for the cause of Christ in India.

True leaders attract followers for two reasons. First of all, they are committed to a cause (and the cause that we have is great). And second, it is readily apparent that a true leader is "all in." That kind of spirit is "catchy." Being involved in a cause makes our lives worth the living.

> Another friend joined our group. His name was Thamby. We became very good friends. He later went to be with the Lord because of an airplane crash. He and I prayed together, and sometimes we would spend all night in prayer, sometimes half the night in prayer pleading and praying for God to provide for our needs, and indeed, God answered our prayers and met our needs.

Prevailing prayer

Have you ever wondered what half the night means?

> We would start about around 9 o'clock in the evening and go till about 1 o'clock in the morning.
>
> Then we would have to be up by 5 o'clock in the morning, but sometimes we would do a whole night on Saturday night. We would start around 10:00 or 10:30 and we would go to around 5 o'clock in the morning.

As G.S. says,

> You really don't understand how soon the time goes
> when you're very engaged in prayer. But many times
> people think prayer is easy. It is not; because it's a
> battle. Your body can be really lenient towards your
> comfort. Prayer is a labor. It's a spiritual labor. We
> really need to cultivate our prayer life; if not we end
> up being kind of lukewarm. So we pray and that
> helps motivate us.

How many missionary books and books about prayer have you read where people spend that kind of time in prayer? Have you ever wondered what they pray for and how they pray?

G.S. said they would pray like this:

> Lord, strengthen us. Give us more spiritual vision.
> Give us open doors, give us hope to light a candle.

We will look more closely at the importance G.S. places on prayer in a later chapter.

He says they would pray for practical things like transportation and food but also for more spiritual power and those kinds of things.

Fasting

G.S. says they would occasionally fast two or three days at a time. Fasting helped them to be more focused as they spent time with the Lord.

They would especially fast as they sought guidance and help from the Lord when facing opposition and conducting evangelistic campaigns.

Every successful business follows a model, and G.S. follows the New Testament model he learned from the Every Home Crusade outreach. And the nights in prevailing prayer formed much of the basis of his later success, and that's coming up soon.

PART 2

**Soul-winning, education, and church-planting ministries—
Training nationals to reach nationals**

CHAPTER 5

Opportunities and opposition

Whatsoever thy hand findeth to do, do it with thy might; for there is no work, nor device, nor knowledge, nor wisdom, in the grave, whither thou goest. (Ecclesiastes 9:10)

Entrepreneurs are opportunity seekers. They act quickly because lots of opportunities are time sensitive. Sometimes they don't have a clear path to follow, but that doesn't stop them from taking on a project. G.S. proved himself to be an entrepreneur right from the outset.

He tells the story of a "business opportunity" at the Bible College. He and his team were broke and they needed to finance their upcoming evangelistic work.

> We prayed and asked the Lord for the money we needed for our Summer Ministry.
>
> *And the Lord answered our prayer. One day I was just waiting, and I heard Dr. Chelli* [Dr. Jacob Chelli was president of Berean Baptist Bible College] talking to a contractor about demolishing a large old building on the campus, removing the debris, and making the ground level.
>
> He quoted a price that Dr. Chelli was unwilling to pay.
>
> So I approached Dr. *Chelli and said I'll do it for half of what he quoted.* He said, "Okay, can you do it?" I said, "Yes, the only thing is, I need the evening off from study hall."

So I took a group of students and we worked for
about six months. That was our first investment in
our ministry.

We earned six thousand rupees and it cost us
around five hundred rupees in expenses. And that
was how we financed our first gospel team. We had
around eight or nine people on the team at that
time.

So G.S. bootstrapped his operation by organizing a team of laborers to
do building demolition. This is reminiscent of the Apostle Paul, who
also financed his own ministry and travel by making tents (Acts 18:3).

By the way, Dr. Chelli had graciously offered G.S. a full scholarship
to Berean. Their relationship grew stronger over the years, and he
became a great supporter of the ministry.

Testing on the field

Like any startup operation involving a team, there's bound to be
some conflict. But it usually doesn't show itself until everybody's
under pressure. G.S. relates the following story:

The gospel team headed off to tell the good news
and to conduct some gospel meetings. A Christian
man who had support from the United States said
that he would provide meals for them. But when we
got there we found out that the "meals" turned out
only to be breakfast.

Even among the eight or nine of us we had very
little money. So we pulled it all together and bought
a little wheat. We mixed it with salt and water and
created "wheat balls."

About the fourth or fifth day when everybody was
really hungry, a couple of fellows nearly got into
fisticuffs because one guy took a larger wheat ball
from another.

I came and found them ready to go at each other. And in order to keep the peace I gave one of the fellows one of my wheat balls. It was worth it to me to be a little hungry and to protect our testimony for the Lord.

But why did this happen? I think the Lord allows struggles such as this to take place so that we will trust more and more in his provision. Sometimes those lessons come at the price of our comfort and even at the cost of our needs. But the lessons are well worthwhile.

Through these things we are shaped according to his desire, and that's what brings glory to the Lord.

The gospel team and development of a brand

Whenever you start a new project, one of the most important things is to name your organization. And that's exactly what G.S. and his fellow missionaries did. In 1976 they started the **Kerala Baptist Gospel Team**, which would eventually become Peoples Baptist Ministries to India (PBMI). Their mission was to preach the gospel in the state of Kerala, located in southern India.

Here's what they did…

We did not go any place to stay, and we just depended upon the Lord and sometimes on my friends. Some of our classmates from college opened up their homes for us to sleep in. We had food that some other people provided for us.

We held meetings, preached the gospel, had Bible studies in different houses, and many people got saved. It was exciting to see so many people trust the Lord Jesus Christ as their Savior. The obvious result was that we had a new church plant in that area.

New converts need to be assembled as a church.

My first church plant was Palghat Fundamental
Baptist Church in the city of Palghat. I stayed in the
area for two weeks holding meetings and preaching
and then had to move on to another area. We started
another church in a city called Tea Plantation as
well.

An early cottage meeting

And still this was just a summer ministry. I was
very highly motivated to go back and minister to
all these new Christians. But I needed to return to
school for my final year.

G.S. graduated from Berean Baptist Bible College and Seminary in
the spring of 1977 with a Bachelor of Religious Education (B.R.E.)
degree. Then he went back to Palghat to minister to the folks there
and to do outreach work.

What made Kerala Baptist Gospel Team different... transitioning into a church planting ministry

What made them different from most teams was their quick integration of church planting into their evangelistic model.

Now this may seem obvious to you, but if you start with a focus of winning people to Christ and it only stays there, you run into the problem of folks who think they're saved but really aren't as well as folks who are saved but never grow.

For example, I am reminded of when I first learned about "The Jesus Film Project."[18] I remember the promotion for the film showing many people in India deeply moved at the crucifixion of the Lord Jesus Christ. Who wouldn't be?

The film has a way of touching the heart. And it's a great tool for evangelism. And many people come to the Lord because of it.

But what then? What about follow-up? What about Bible doctrine? And what about discipleship?

The New Testament model is that believers must be assembled in local churches. It is there that believers are followed up and taught Bible doctrine and proper Christian deportment. It is through the local church that disciples are made.

Consider the Apostle Paul, who sometimes stayed in one place for a year or year and a half just to fully ground the local church.

It's not just enough that people are born into the family of God. The secret of a successful and victorious Christian life is birth-growth-maturity. That is the ministry of the local church and its leadership.

A mature Christian is conscientious about winning others to Christ. If our Lord's kingdom is to expand, then instilling the desire to win lost souls to the Lord Jesus Christ must be woven into the fabric of the local church.

18   The Jesus Film Project. Available at: http://www.jesusfilm.org/nda/grants/gamo-jesus-film-project

The culture in India is rapidly changing just like it did in the United States fifty plus years ago. Right now people are hungry for the truth. Now is the day of salvation while they are open to receiving it. The time is coming when the folks there will care as little as most of the folks here.

A Bible Institute is needed

G.S. and his team soon realized that the harvest was truly great, so they began to pray the Lord of the harvest to bring more laborers into the field. And it was in 1978 that they realized they needed to establish a Bible Institute to train those laborers whom the Lord would send.

> *Pray ye therefore the Lord of the harvest, that he will send forth labourers into his harvest. (Matthew 9:38).*

They made converts. Great. But the Lord is looking for disciples, not just converts.

What to do?

The only way converts become disciples is by being taught to follow the Lord.

They were doing step 1: Going and preaching

> *And he said unto them, Go ye into all the world, and* **preach the gospel** *to every creature. (Mark 16:15)*

And

> *Go ye therefore, and* **teach all nations**, **baptizing** *them in the name of the Father, and of the Son, and of the Holy Ghost. (Matthew 28:19)*

A team of workers baptizes new converts in a local body of water.

They taught about the true God and about the Savior of all men, the Lord Jesus Christ. They also baptized believers...

But the children of the Kingdom needed to grow into maturity...

They were doing step 2: Establishing churches

Teaching them to observe *all things whatsoever I have commanded you: and, lo, I am with you alway, even unto the end of the world. Amen. (Matthew 28:20)*

They established local churches to teach them to observe all things whatsoever the Lord has commanded.

But they needed to do step 3: Training faithful men

Like Paul told Timothy...

And the things that thou hast heard of me among many witnesses, the same **commit thou to faithful men, who shall be able to teach others** *also. (2 Timothy 2:2)*

Enter entrepreneurial thinking. They were successful evangelists and had planted a few churches. Now it was time to scale the operation.

They needed to multiply themselves. They needed to establish a school.

In 1978 we were praying and praying and praying, and God put on our hearts the desire to start a small Bible Institute. But how were we going to afford to do this?

The same way they did everything else. Trust in the Lord to provide the daily needs and the funds necessary to operate such an enterprise. G.S. didn't allow the lack of funds to stop the project. They prayed and the Lord provided. They knew that the Lord had laid upon their hearts to start the Bible Institute for his glory.

A Bible Institute is established

Our prayer was answered in 1980 when we started a small Bible Institute. It was located about eighty kilometers northwest of Trivandrum in the city of Oyoor, Kerala, in a rented building in association with a church plant there.

At the beginning we had seven to ten students. We did not charge any tuition. Many could not afford it anyway. The students actually camped out near the rented building, but they were hungry for the Word of God and that was what was most important. We called the school Berean Baptist Bible Institute.

We stayed there only eight months, and in the latter part of 1980 we moved the location of the Bible Institute to another rented building, this time in Trivandrum. This is where we planted Peoples Baptist Church. All the ministries we do today are under the auspices of this church.

Students meeting in one of the first classrooms at the Bible Institute

We rented there up until 1985 when we were able to purchase one-third acre of land. We've been there for over thirty years; that's where the Bible College and Seminary is now.

We still don't charge any tuition but take an offering from those who can afford to contribute to the work. We don't have tuition because it is more important to have the right kind of student whether or not he can pay for his education and boarding.

The actual cost for room and board at the college as of 2015 is $95. The students are made aware of this cost even though they can't pay it so that they can appreciate the **value** of what they are receiving. A successful organization needs people who are sold out to the cause. Those are the people you make an investment in, and that's exactly what G.S. and his team do.

The Bible Institute becomes a Bible College

As time went on they upgraded the operation from a Bible Institute to a Bible College and changed the standard language from Malayalam (the native tongue in Kerala State) to English because their vision broadened from Kerala State to the whole of India.

That was in 1985. The new Bible College began to expand slowly, and through contributions of many of God's people, pieces of land were bought and buildings were built little by little. Here a little, there a little—one thing led to another—and God's hand was on it all the time.

The first kitchen

The old boy's dormitory

The theme of the ministry is "Little is much when God is in it."[19]

---

19   Kittie L. Suffield, "Little Is Much When God Is in It" (1924). Kittie accompanied George Beverly Shea in his first public solo at a camp meeting, encouraging him to sing another solo in a lower key after his voice cracked and he resolved to never sing in public again. (Nelson Bradford, Naznet.com, posted December 6, 2010. Available at: http://www.naznet.com/community/showthread.php/2976-quot-Little-is-Much-When-God-Is-in-It-quot) (accessed October 21, 2015).

Today Peoples Baptist Bible College and Seminary continues to train young men and women to carry on and carry out the Great Commission. You can visit their website at http://www.pbbcs.org/.

Opposition

Like former boxing heavyweight champion Mike Tyson once said: "Everybody has a plan until they get punched in the mouth."[20]

All entrepreneurs learn how to roll with the punches so to speak. And the same is true for Brother G.S. Planning is important. But sometimes plans change, and in the ministry and in our lives we have to assume the Lord is in it and be ready to change.

> We had some opposition when we bought land for our first Bible College in 1986. It was actually southwest of Trivandrum. We started work constructing temporary buildings when a group of Hindu men came and beat up some of our pastors working there.
>
> I got word of it, hopped on my bike, and headed out there. Some people stopped me on the way.
>
> "Don't go there because of rioters." I had already spent one week of continual prayer because of all the money that we had invested there. Now I couldn't do anything. It was a heavy burden for me. I could not sleep.
>
> One morning God really strengthened my heart to go to that area. Around fifty to sixty people gathered there ready to beat me up. They said, "This is the leader." Somehow God gave me strength. I just went near, got out of the car, and said, "I don't think you understand."

20   Mike Bernardino, "Mike Tyson Explains One of His Most Famous Quotes," *Sun Sentinel*, November 9, 2012. Available online: http://articles.sun-sentinel.com/2012-11-09/sports/sfl-mike-tyson-explains-one-of-his-most-famous-quotes-20121109_1_mike-tyson-undisputed-truth-famous-quotes (accessed August 21, 2015).

"We just want to have a Bible College over here, but if you fellows don't want one, I'm not going to start one here. I will sell this property if somebody wants to buy it." One individual jumped up and said, "I will buy."

Proverbs 16:7: *When a man's ways please the LORD, he maketh even his enemies to be at peace with him.*

Romans 12:18: *If it be possible, as much as lieth in you, live peaceably with all men.*

That was an answer to prayer. People came to beat me up, but I sold the property instead. I was so excited. I made an agreement with the man, then my tears began to flow and I went away rejoicing.

The Bible College needed to reopen. I had purchased one-third of an acre for a local church at another location. It's just opposite of the city, just in the surrounding hills. We bought the land, and that's where our current campus is located to this day.

An early chapel building

I took some of the pastors and we worked for nearly two weeks to completely level the place. We dug the well, put in a temporary building, and within twelve days we started classes.

So with a Bible College and a couple of church plants established, it was time for the missionary-entrepreneur to teach others his model...

CHAPTER 6

The soul-winning, church-planting model taught at the Bible Colleges and Seminary

The fruit of the righteous is a tree of life; and he that winneth souls is wise. (Proverbs 11:30)

Our model is the New Testament model; our Master's model; no new gimmicks—a passion for souls, reach them with the gospel, disciple them and motivate them to meet others' needs both physically and spiritually.

The New Testament model is found in the book of Acts where it clearly states that the mission includes three foundational activities:

1. **Teaching, preaching, and soul winning:** *...in every house, they ceased not to teach and preach Jesus Christ (Acts 5:42),* which is the ministry of the Word (Acts 6:4). The apostles taught believers to become disciples so that they can bring others to a saving knowledge of our Lord Jesus Christ.

2. **Prayer:** *But we will give ourselves continually to prayer, and to the ministry of the word. (Acts 6:4)*

3. **Humanitarian works:** referred to as "daily ministration," these works include taking care of widows and other people in need and is further defined in the book of James.

And in those days, when the number of the disciples was multiplied, there arose a murmuring of the Grecians against the Hebrews, because their widows were neglected in the daily ministration. (Acts 6:1)

Pure religion and undefiled before God and the Father is this, To visit the fatherless and widows in their affliction, and to keep himself unspotted from the world.
(James 1:27)

And then there's the "secret sauce" of Kingdom expansion…

Church-planting summer ministries

The model that has worked for G.S. for nearly forty years is the **Summer Outreach Ministry**.

Instead of going home for summer break, many of the students and all faculty members serve with evangelistic teams striving to reach every state of India. Typically, about thirty teams are sent out with eleven students and one faculty member in each team.

A Summer Outreach Ministry team heading to the field

Everywhere they go they:

- Invite people to gospel meetings through door-to-door evangelism.
- Hand out hundreds of thousands of tracts per summer.
- Hold open-air meetings, leading to cottage meetings and Bible studies.
- Preach, sing, and give testimonies at evangelistic meetings.
- Deal one-on-one with inquirers, seeking to lead them to Christ.
- Do follow-up work, which results in Bible studies, baptism of new converts, establishing new churches, and motivating them to reach their communities with the Gospel.

Through these God-given efforts, more than 2,700 churches in twenty-nine states of India have been founded. In addition, eighty churches have been established in three neighboring countries.

These churches are composed of over 250,000 souls. Home Bible studies are continually being conducted in preparation for becoming newly organized local assemblies. Plans are also being made to enter Bangladesh, Sri Lanka, Pakistan, and other countries.

> The Summer Outreach Ministry not only brings souls to the Lord Jesus but also bonds the students with each other and with the faculty members who join them.

An outreach team sets up speakers for an open-air meeting in Kerala State.

Plus the students establish friendships with the people in whatever area they go to. This creates affection toward that particular area so they'll think about it as they come back to the college, and then maybe next year they'll get the chance to go there again.

That way their burden for those people will grow deeper, and after graduation they might take the leading of the Lord to go there in service to him.

At the same time, the faculty who went into the field with the students will not only be able to see the work and give guidance to the students for teaching or ministry but also will be excited about the souls that are saved and they'll come back and motivate the students in the classroom with great enthusiasm. Both the faculty and students get practical experience. So not only does the Summer Ministry win souls, but also we are actually preparing future workers to go to the field.

G.S. Nair and a team member preach at an evangelistic meeting.

An outreach team attracts a crowd in northeast India.

We send out girls' teams also but not with the men. The girls go out and work with the schools teaching English, helping in children's homes and vocational training centers, and serving in other areas. We have maybe five or six teams of girls with each team consisting of five to seven girls and a pastor and his wife.

We take care of transportation and necessities, and the hosting pastors and churches provide meals. The girls contribute some money for meals if they can afford it. This gives the local church the opportunity to send these "missionaries" into the field in their own areas.

Bible College Extension Schools

The first extension school started in 1984.

There are 15 schools located in nine different states: Tamil Nadu, Karnataka, Orissa, Andhra, Telangana, Manipur, Punjab, UP and in Myanmar and Nepal. They teach over 230 students. This work-study program offers an eight-week course spread over two years for men who work and can't afford to travel or attend full-time at a Bible College.

Students eager to learn at an extension school in Telangana State

G.S. Nair visiting an extension school in Andra Pradesh

Peoples Baptist Seminary

In the years that followed, the ministry experienced lots of growth. By 1990 the Bible College added a Seminary and offered a Doctor of Divinity degree. The other two Bible Colleges are located in the states of Punjab (northern India) and Chhattisgarh (central India). The schools have only one purpose: to lead nationals to the Word of God and to train and motivate them to win souls, make disciples, and mature the saints by planting churches thereby fulfilling the Great Commission.

Four views of the campus today; note the men's dormitory and dining hall in the upper left.

Peoples Baptist Bible College and Seminary graduating class of 2015

The 2015 graduating class from the college in Kerala State

Private Schools

PBMI oversees six private schools (five in India and one in Nepal) with an enrollment of over 600 students. They are not labeled as "Christian" but rather "private." This gives the opportunity to present the gospel in an unencumbered way.

Many non-Christian parents send their children to these schools because of the quality education their children receive. Hundreds of children and many of their parents have come to know the Lord through this outreach. Recently, one of the schools in Manipur State conducted a youth camp (one of many) where forty young people came to know the Lord. This school is also teaching seventeen orphans from their nearby children's home.

A private school in Orissa where children hear the gospel

Women's Ministry Vocational Training Centers

There are two centers offering a two-year course to train female nationals to do the work of the ministry.

Some parts of Indian culture (and groups) forbid a man to speak to an unfamiliar woman, making it difficult for pastors to communicate the gospel to women. To overcome this problem, they train young women for missionary work among the women and children of India. They are taught church-related ministries such as orphan work and teaching in Vacation Bible Schools and Christian grade schools.

Through vocational training in housekeeping, sewing, knitting, and embroidering, women are taught life-sustaining skills and the means to spread the gospel as they teach others. Upon graduation each woman is given a sewing machine. This is a valuable resource for earning income and sharing the gospel. For example, through this means three churches were planted in three different villages.

And speaking of women in the ministry, I'm happy to introduce you to the lady that stands behind the missionary-entrepreneur of India...

CHAPTER 7

Sarah Nair—The perfect helpmeet

Who can find a virtuous woman? for her price is far above rubies. (Proverbs 31:10)

"You think only you have faith? I trust the Lord too"—Sarah Nair

They say that "behind every great man there's an even greater woman." And such a woman is G.S. Nair's wife, Sarah.[21]

Sarah Nair

Sarah joins a list of other missionary wives like:

Ann Hasseltine Judson (1789–1826), the wife of Adoniram Judson (1788–1850), known as America's first foreign missionary. The Judsons' labor in Burma is the stuff of many a biography. Working alongside her husband, Ann translated portions of the Bible into Burmese and Thai, wrote a catechism in Burmese, and wrote of missionary life in the field. It has been said that "her work and writings made 'the role of missionary wife as a calling' legitimate for 19th century Americans."[22]

---

21   I am indebted to Mathan Kurian, a friend of the Nairs, for suggesting the chapter title and providing background information on Sarah Nair's marriage and ministry. Quotes are from Mathan Kurian, personal communication, August 28, 2015.

22   "Ann Hasseltine Judson," Wikipedia, last modified August 27, 2015, quoting Dana L. Robert, "The Mother of Modern Missions," *Christian History & Biography* 90: 22–24. Available online: https://en.wikipedia.org/wiki/Ann_Hasseltine_Judson

Maria Taylor (1837–1870), the wife of Hudson Taylor (1832–1905), famous missionary to China. She is known as the "Mother" of the China Inland Mission, proving herself to be "an invaluable assistant and influence" to her husband. Her grave marker reads, in part, "an earnest Christian and devoted missionary, a faithful and affectionate wife and tender mother, a sincere and warm hearted friend, to her to live was Christ, and to die was gain." [23]

Elisabeth Elliot (1926–2015), a famous Christian author and speaker and missionary wife of Jim Elliot, who was killed in 1956 while attempting to make missionary contact with the Auca Indians of eastern Ecuador. Elisabeth later went to live with the Auca for two years, sharing with them the gospel for which her husband had died. [24]

Rosalind Goforth (1864–1942), wife of Jonathan Goforth (1859–1936). Together they served God in Manchuria and China. In 1900 the Goforths had to flee for many miles across China during the Boxer Rebellion. Five of their eleven children died very young. Rosalind wrote four books, including *How I Know God Answers Prayer* (1921) and *Climbing: Memoirs of a Missionary's Wife* (1940). [25]

The life of a missionary wife is a life of sacrifice, and Sarah Nair has made her share of sacrifices.

---

23 "Maria Jane Taylor," Wikipedia, last modified June 6, 2015. Available online: https://en.wikipedia.org/wiki/Maria_Jane_Taylor

24 "Elisabeth Elliot," Wikipedia, last modified August 21, 2015. Available online: https://en.wikipedia.org/wiki/Elisabeth_Elliot

25 "Rosalind Goforth," Wikipedia, last modified May 17, 2015. Available online: https://en.wikipedia.org/wiki/Rosalind_Goforth

Sarah was born into a nominal Christian family. She was seventh of nine siblings, all of whom live in America. Sarah, her mother, and three siblings were converted under the ministry of Brother G.S. Sarah was considering migrating to the United States but the Lord touched her heart (and so did G.S. Nair).

As the relationship grew, G.S. made her aware of the enormous cost associated with the ministry. He didn't have much money and there were great demands on his time even in the early days. He was sold out to the cause. This can be a major source of frustration for a wife and mother.

G.S. tried to discourage her from marriage to him because of his lack of income, his excommunication from his parents because of the gospel, his lack even of housing.

Her family was relatively well-to-do, from an aristocratic Knanaya background, and a union with him would mean sacrifice and, more importantly, trusting the Lord to meet their needs.

It wouldn't be easy. Was she prepared for such a commitment?

She said to him, "You think only you have faith? I trust the Lord too."

Dr. Jacob Chelli married G.S. and Sarah in 1978. Her life was woven into the fabric of the ministry from the first day of marriage. G.S. cites many occasions when she would pray night after night seeking God in faith and bearing heavy burdens and needs, but like he says, "She is always with me and encouraging me. She never gives up, and she's always faithful."

Sarah Nair as a young bride

Because G.S. travels extensively Sarah was often home alone caring for their four children. Mathan Kurian,[26] a close family friend, notes that Sarah displayed great "patience in bringing them up and nurturing them in a godly way." Her daughter Debee Johnson says, "She has sacrificed a lot of her time with Dad so that he could travel and preach. I believe that Dad couldn't have done so much without this support from Mother." Each of the Nair children love the Lord and serve in ministry either directly or indirectly today.

The ministry has grown and turned out to be so expansive that sometimes Sarah takes the phone calls that G.S. would get. There have been as many as eighty to ninety calls in one day! Mr. Kurian says, "Sarah's calmness of character, meek and quiet spirit, even in the midst of difficulties should be highly appreciated ... She has a unique talent in handling people with different difficulties."

> *... even the ornament of a meek and quiet spirit, which is in the sight of God of great price. (1 Peter 3:4b)*

---

26   Rev. Mathan K. Kurian is Academic Dean of Peoples Baptist Bible College and Seminary. He has been associated with the ministry for twenty-one years.

G.S. and Sarah with their four young children circa 1998
(from left to right): Debee, Suzaan, Timothy, and Dawn

Because of his position, G.S. and Sarah accommodate lots (and lots) of visitors to their home for counsel, encouragement, and fellowship.

And being given to hospitality, Sarah has prepared and served lots (and lots) of meals in her home. As is the custom, she always sees that her guests are all fed before she eats. "Her hospitality is sweet and admirable" and she is "the backbone" of her husband and ministry, according to Mr. Kurian.

Plus, she is a great encourager for pastor's wives. Mr. Kurian describes her as a "caring sister, praying woman, praise-worthy and beautiful." She has a special burden for the poor and orphans. She helps plan, organize, and implement women's meetings, takes care of certain matters regarding children's homes, and also teaches Home Economics to the girls in the college.

Her daughter Debee also says, "As Dad travels a lots she had the big responsibility of bringing up us kids as well as looking after the Ministry's financial and administrative works. When Dad's home, we get lots of visitors and most of the time have to feed them too. She always sees that they are all fed before she eats."

"She is kind, considerate, and listens to us and is always there for her kids. She is also a quiet person; a woman of prayer who encourages other women to pray, and has a great faith in her Savior. As a mother there is not a better role model than she."

Her daughter Dawn says, "Mommy has been that pillar of strength for the family through multiple trials and problems the family has gone through. She derives strength from God and faithfully believes in everything that God will see us through."

"I can remember the days she would give that last bit she had because she believed someone else has it worse than her. No matter who it is, whether it's someone who has hurt her in their actions or their words, she turns around and forgives them, and I have seen time and again how she would help them when they are in need."

And here are some comments from her youngest daughter, Suzaan:

"In every situation in my life I would try to think and act like my Mom, but it's hard because I can never be half the person my Mom is. Her patience, generosity, and faith, her devotion to her family, her inner strength, and her humbleness and willingness to serve the Lord are some of the characteristics I wish and try to develop in me. She is the perfect example of the Proverbs 31 woman."

"My Mommy led me to the Lord at the age of four and sowed the seeds of reading the Bible and praying in all of us at a young age."

"Mommy has been a great support for the ladies at church and in the ministry. She is always ready to give them her time and effort, even if she would not have time for herself. She always puts other people and their needs first before hers."

"Daddy and Mommy are like two sides of the same coin. Many times I have woken up to my parents on their knees praying, no matter what time it is. They go over and beyond to help and pray for everyone, not expecting anything in return. I could not have asked for more godly parents."

Her son Timothy describes his mother this way: "Mom is a great reflection of what it means to be a godly mother. I couldn't be more blessed than to have such a mother. She has stood by me during the high and low tides of my life with the same kind of unconditional love that the Lord has for His children. She has inspired me tremendously to serve others rather than being served."

Mr. Kurian sees Sarah as "the perfect helpmeet" enabling G.S. to "go forward on his Father's business."

The Nair family celebrates their daughter's wedding in 2011. From left to right: daughter Dawn holds Stephen, Sunil (Dawn's husband); in front of G.S. are grandsons Benjamin and Jonathan; the bride and groom, Suzaan and Jay, with another grandson Jabez; Sarah; son Timothy; Johnson (Debee's husband) and daughter Debee.

CHAPTER 8

The gates of hell fight back—Demon experiences in India

And I say also unto thee, That thou art Peter, and upon this rock I will build my church; and the gates of hell shall not prevail against it. (Matthew 16:18)

Competition

Every entrepreneur faces it, but it's the unseen competition we have as Christians that can be the most daunting. The more you work for the Lord, the more intense the opposition can become.

It's been said that Martin Luther while at Wartburg was translating the Bible, the Devil came to visit him. Satan, who was vehemently opposed to the divine mission of the great reformer, sought to tempt him and thwart the work. In response, Luther grabbed the inkwell from which he was writing and threw it at the Evil One's head. For many years, tourists who visited the study of Martin Luther at Wartburg Castle were shown the ink stain on the wall that supposedly occurred when Luther threw the ink pot.[27]

While some question whether that particular story is true, no doubt Martin Luther faced his share of opposition, just as the Apostle Paul had, and just as the ministry of G.S. Nair in India has.

---

27   Mark Creech, "The Night the Demon Visited," *Christian Post*, May 14, 2013. Available online: http://www.christianpost.com/news/the-night-the-demon-visited-95804/#DKO5MsCxxTl89tEp.99 (accessed August 21, 2015).

Targets of a death threat

A man called him and on the phone and told him where his children were and that they were going to be killed. There was really no way to defend against this kind of thing, so G.S. ultimately moved his family from Trivandrum to Bangalore (and started a church there in his spare time).

Five years later, G.S. learned that the person who had called him had committed suicide. Another one who was involved in the plot was murdered and the third died in an accident.

Over time a couple of believers have been killed, pastors have been beaten up, and three or four churches have been burned. All these attacks were by militant anti-Christian elements.

There is a price to pay when one chooses to be a Christian in India. For example, G.S. tells the story of one of his associated pastors who was sick. G.S. went to visit him in the hospital:

> As I prayed the pastor reached out to hold my hand and said, "Pastor, you came all the way from Trivandrum to visit me." He was in Mangalore [over 600 kilometers away]. He said, "My father and mother live only thirty kilometers away from me and yet never come to visit because I'm a Christian."

Sometimes the Christians are totally cut off from their families because of their faith in the Lord Jesus Christ.

Opposition in the spirit realm

They say there are 330 million gods in Hinduism, the main religion of India. No one has ever named them all, but one thing is for sure; when you have a nation full of so many idols and the belief that there are that many gods, it provides fertile ground for the devils to play games on and oppress the children of men.[28]

---

28   While there is much discussion in Christian circles about whether believers can be possessed or merely oppressed, this chapter generally uses the term "possession" without trying to weigh in on the debate.

G.S. has had many experiences in dealing with devils. He says that in some cities and towns you can literally feel the oppression of our enemy. We will cover a few of his experiences here, but first some background.

In 1960 Moody Press published a book called *Demon Experiences in Many Lands: Strange Occurrences in Mission Fields of the World, A Compilation*. I got ahold of the book shortly after I was saved in 1978.

Demon Experiences in Many Lands *is a compilation of demotic experiences on the mission field.*

I had always been interested in ghosts and extraterrestrials before I got saved. But it was only after I got saved that I understood who and what they really were.

And then after reading and, more importantly, believing the Bible, I came to see that God had competition. The Devil is real and devils are real.

We've all read stories in the Scripture of how devils possessed people and the things that they did. It's enough to make you not want to get involved with them.

And yet people do all the time.

They go to fortune-tellers, play with Ouija boards and occult materials, and expose themselves to satanically oriented music and movies. They even unwittingly make signs and symbols that represent Satanism and witchcraft: things like pentagrams, Baphomet, hexagrams, the All-Seeing Eye (on the back of a one dollar bill, no less), an inverted cross, the goat head, and so on.

It seems that popular culture is well on its way to accepting the devil as their god.

There are lots of interesting stories in *Demon Experiences in Many Lands*, including a whole chapter about demon possession in India. The book describes a symposium on demonology that was held in Madras (now called Chennai), India.

Their purpose was to collect views on the topic of demonology. They understood that demons have the power to afflict men with diseases and mental derangement.

The first interviewed was Mr. N. Daniel, founder of the Laymen's Evangelical Fellowship. They asked him if he'd ever seen a person possessed with demons.

He answered, "Yes, hundreds of them in countries where there are idol worship and spirit worship, it is not difficult to find people who are possessed with demons. China and India are among the worst places for this.... **In India more women are possessed than men**"[29]

I found that to be an interesting statement. Why more women than men?

I'm not sure anybody really knows except that maybe a woman's spirit is more susceptible for some reason.

---

29   Elijah Bingham et al., *Demon Experiences in Many Lands: Strange Occurrences in Mission Fields of the World, A Compilation* (Chicago: Moody Press, 1960), p. 20.

How does G.S. know a person is demon possessed?

> They act like demons. It's not a physical thing. We
> can tell by their appearance. We can see how that
> they strike the meeting screaming like they're filled
> with a ghost. Usually, we claim the name of Jesus
> Christ and cast them out.

Mr. Daniel from India said the same thing. "In our meetings of revival
types those demons come out as in the time of Jesus. Either they
shout, cry or weep aloud, or fall down"[30] And how do they handle
the situation? "We rebuke the demons in the name of Christ....
In most cases they come out promptly. But the one who uses the
name of Christ must be strong in faith, clean in heart, with a pure
conscience. One ought to be very careful about his own personal
faith and character."[31]

Notice how he says that one ought to be very careful about his own
personal faith and character. I've known G.S. Nair for nearly thirty-
five years, and his personal faith and character is what has impressed
me about him over that time.

Demons and inanimate objects

Mr. Daniel tells us about how demons can inhabit inanimate objects.
Here's what he said:

> Some people who occupy houses, where evil spirits have
> worshiped for many years, are afflicted by those evil spirits.
> Sickness, heart trouble, stomach pain, fever and all sorts of
> things will come upon them. Then somebody must rebuke
> those evil spirits.
>
> Sometimes there are idols. Behind these idols are evil spirits.
> Sometimes a portion of the wall is marked out for pictures to
> be worshiped. These pictures must be scraped off, the wall

---

30   Ibid, p. 20.

31   Ibid.

must be whitewashed and the man of God must pray. When God takes us to such homes they are permanently relieved of all those troubles.[32]

G.S. shares an experience he and a team member had in one meeting...

> We were conducting a small meeting. Mathai was with me. I was preaching the Word of God to around forty-five people who had gathered in that house.

It's interesting that G.S. calls a meeting of forty-five people small, isn't it?

> As we were concluding the meeting and giving a gospel invitation, a girl that was possessed by a demon started just rolling over on the ground. Her hair was completely disheveled and her face was different.
>
> So I just walked down to her. I am very careful, I don't touch them. I don't lay my hand on them, and that's because it's a biblical standard. I always follow that. And I said, "In the name of Jesus Christ, keep quiet." Immediately, she was like a dead body. She didn't move. I went back and continued my invitation. Around seven or eight people got saved.
>
> Then finally I just moved back to deal with the girl. I asked the owner of the house to pour some water on her and she woke up like she was getting up from sleep. Then I shared the gospel with her and led her to the Lord Jesus Christ.
>
> I strongly believe, you just don't cast out demons, you need to lead the person to the Lord Jesus Christ. Because if you don't, it can be worse than the first state. So I led her to the Lord Jesus Christ.

---

32   Ibid, p. 23.

So Mathai and others from our team went to our vehicle to go home. I put the key in and the vehicle would not start. So we tried to jumpstart it by pushing it. We couldn't push the vehicle. Eight men were pushing and the vehicle would not move.

We tried everything. We even looked underneath to see if there was anything holding it back. Nothing was there. And it was in neutral, not in gear. And it wasn't a problem with the power steering.

And then I told Mathai, "I know what is happening. Let us pray." I claimed the victory and cast out demons from the surroundings, you know. Next thing, it started to work. I don't have any explanation of how the devil possessed the vehicle, but it happened.

I know what you're thinking; you've probably felt like you owned a car that was possessed.

It's a good thing you don't live in India—you could be right!

Anyway, Mr. Daniel from India relates this story: "One woman, out of mere enthusiasm and loyalty to the Christian religion, broke an idol. Immediately an evil spirit possessed her. She was brought to me. The evil spirit said 'she broke my idol. That is why I possessed her.' I drove out the devil. But her home was not established in the faith. Evidently there is hidden sin in some hearts. I have heard that the devil sometimes returns."[33]

---

33 Ibid, p. 23.

A demon-possessed pastor's daughter

G.S. and another team member had another encounter:

> One day Phillip and I had a demon-possession experience with another pastor's daughter. This pastor told me his daughter had gotten possessed up north in India while she was working there. They were working in an area where there were a lot of Hindu black magicians operating. They came back with the problem. The girl was demon-possessed.
>
> The pastor called me, and I went and visited this girl and her husband. She was very quiet when I went to speak with her. The pastor wanted me to lay hands upon her and pray. I would not do that, but I prayed. Everything went well.
>
> That night I went home, which was around fifty miles away. At half past midnight I was in prayer. Suddenly something just went over my head. It didn't touch my head, but I knew something had gone by. And suddenly the lights went out. I was scared
>
> After a few minutes, the lights came back on. I was sweating because I got really scared. I was praying all that time, but I knew something just went over my head. It's not of God, I knew that.
>
> The next day the pastor came to my home in the morning. He was shaken and said, "Last night my daughter was completely possessed by demons, we could not sleep, and Pastor, you have to come."
>
> "She says that when you prayed the power [i.e., the demon] would stand away from her." The devil told her parents, "Now I am going to show you my power." I asked, "What was the time?" They said 12:30 a.m.

Apparently the demons did a "flyover" as G.S. was praying, just to show off their power. It seems like the midnight hour is an important time for devils.

Mr. Daniel also said, "Demons are very vengeful. They will always try to attack a person who wants to drive them out. They do not want to leave. When we send them out they become terribly afraid, because they know their future, that they will have to go to a place where they will have to burn. Sometimes when we place our hands on demon possessed persons they shout, 'I am burning, I am burning, I am in hell.'"[34]

Here are a couple of other excerpts from *Demon Experiences in Many Lands*.

> There was girl who was demon possessed in Colombia, "a curious thing we observed at that time was that if we stayed with her until about midnight the demons didn't return any more that night." [35]

> And there was a 17-year-old young man who was possessed in a Mexican village named Fernando. His attacks came usually about dusk and lasted well on toward midnight.[36]

A few more comments about devils

Mr. Daniel said that the demons "are generally very stubborn and refused to speak; but we that are in the Lord may command them to open their mouths. I often ask them who is Lord of heaven. They tell me it is the Lord Jesus Christ and acknowledge that there is a heaven and hell, and tell many things about these places. We have complete control over these demons by the wonderful name of Jesus Christ." [37]

---

34   Ibid, p. 29.

35   Ibid, p. 44.

36   Ibid, p. 49.

37   Ibid, p. 31.

You may be interested to know that Mr. Daniel also said that the devils "believe the Scriptures and when we read the Scriptures in their presence they tremble and when we read Luke 10:18, 19 they are terribly afraid." [38]

> **Luke 10:18–19:** *And he said unto them, I beheld Satan as lightning fall from heaven. Behold, I give unto you power to tread on serpents and scorpions, and over all the power of the enemy: and nothing shall by any means hurt you.*

He also said that the devils recognize Jesus Christ as Lord of all and "they won't tell any lies about him. They are terribly afraid when you even mention the name of Christ, and they would like to close their ears from hearing his name."[39]

Paul V. Gupta, the first president of the Hindustan Bible Institute, in Chennai, said he had known devils to speak in different languages—which is an interesting comment when you consider how widespread the use of "tongues" is today.

Dr. Gupta goes on to also offer this piece of advice:

> Unless you bind the powers of darkness through prayer and through the strengthening of the blood of Jesus, you cannot preach the gospel with as good results. In India I have seen many conversions take place when demons were cast out. Hindus are very much afflicted by these demons.... Behind every idol there is a devil.[40]

---

38   Ibid, p. 31.

39   Ibid, p. 31.

40   Ibid, p. 36.

Dr. Gupta also explains about having the power to cast out demons...

> Fasting and prayer are a great help. These two ways are hard,
> but they can bring us closer to the Lord Jesus Christ so that
> we become deeply conscious that we have a power; and we
> go with that power and exalt Jesus Christ. Fasting and prayer
> are very essential to bind the powers of darkness, and to cast
> out devils.[41]

Despite earthly and spiritual opposition, the ministry continues to
seek new opportunities to win souls to Christ, including through
humanitarian outreaches...

---

41   Ibid. p. 36.

PART 3

Evangelistic humanitarian ministries—
Evangelism is "in" everything they do

CHAPTER 9

Humanitarian evangelism

*But whoso hath this world's good, and seeth his brother
have need, and shutteth up his bowels of compassion from
him, how dwelleth the love of God in him? (1 John 3:17)*

There are lots of poor and destitute people in India. The unemployment
rate is really high as well. But there's also a caste and religious
system that doesn't help. After all, if someone is working out their
bad karma from a previous lifetime, why should you get in the way
by performing works of charity toward them?

But our Lord is full of compassion. And so is G.S. As a result, over
the years PBMI has established twenty orphanages, a home for
abused girls, a ministry to lepers, and other outreaches to do corporal
works of mercy.

The Tsunami Home Story

G.S. relates this touching story of a girl who spent most of her life
at one of the children's homes. She was orphaned in the terrible
tsunami of 2004.

We had a young girl who grew up in our tsunami children's home.
She lost both her parents in the 2004 tsunami but she was saved
at our home. In 2014 I went to the home because we were quickly
running out of funding. I spoke to the children and told them of our
situation.

> She said, "Thank you for my education, my home,
> everything, but please don't close the tsunami
> home, because others need it."

That touched my heart because I saw the heart she had for others. And I needed to find a way to keep this home open. So I brought the need before God's people, and we were able to raise enough funds to keep it open until the end of December 2015.

Soul winning is the motivation for the humanitarian work that we do. If they come to know Christ, then we motivate them to tell other needy people so they can know the Lord.

The tsunami children's home

While I was studying in Bible College, I used to read one biography a month. One of them was about William Booth. He was the founder of the Salvation Army. His battle cry was "Others!" I was motivated by his statement. But we must have a balance. We never, ever put humanitarian work in front of the gospel. The gospel must be first.

And we do many humanitarian works. But they are all evangelistic. The example is what our Lord did with the five loaves of bread and the fishes. He could have satisfied the people without even using his disciples, but he didn't. He broke the bread and gave it to his disciples and the disciples gave it to the people. He's teaching us that you're there to meet the needs of others with him as the source. Like the Scripture says:

Thou openest thine hand, and satisfiest the desire of every living thing. (Psalms 145:16)

And that's what their ministry does. Like they say, "Evangelism isn't all we do but it's 'in' everything we do."

Take a look at other examples of the gospel in action.

Children's Homes

Children are loved and nurtured in PBMI homes; here in Jagdalpur, Chhattisgarh State.

G.S. and PBMI founded and run twenty children's homes. Some call them orphanages.

But they don't. That's because the children are cared for by a pastor, his wife, and members of a local church. They don't see the children as "orphaned" anymore. They are members of a family. And lots of these kids come to know the Lord Jesus Christ as their own Savior.

PBMI children's home in Haldwani, Uttarakhand State

Right now (2015) they care for 490 children.

They don't go looking for orphans. There are plenty of them. So how do they decide where to establish a children's home? First a pastor and his wife must feel a special call from the Lord to care for the fatherless.

PBMI children's home in Irenepuram, Tamil Nadu State

Then, through the outreach of the local church, as they come across needy children, they prayerfully look into the matter of starting a children's home. If they truly feel called of the Lord to do this ministry, they are carefully trained and qualified for the work.

PBMI children's homes in (top) Uravakonda, Andhra Pradesh State, and (bottom) Chembur, Trivandrum District, Kerala State

Like the Scripture teaches:

> *Pure religion and undefiled before God and the Father is this, To visit the fatherless and widows in their affliction, and to keep himself unspotted from the world.*
>
> *(James 1:27)*

PBMI children's home in Kanyakumari District, Tamil Nadu State

Peoples Baptist Girls Home—An answer to human trafficking

Human trafficking is the trade of humans, most commonly for the purpose of sexual slavery, forced labor, or commercial sexual exploitation.

It certainly is in the headlines today. Young children, both boys and girls, are used, abused, and sold. It's a worldwide form of wickedness. And it happens in India too.

But it's not surprising, for the Scripture says:

> *And we know that we are of God, and the whole world lieth in wickedness. (1 John 5:19)*

Kevin Bales, author of ***Disposable People*** (2004), estimates that as many as 27 million people are in "modern-day slavery" around the world. A 2008 International Labour Organization (ILO) study estimated that women and girls make up 98 percent of those trafficked for commercial sex.[42]

---

42   Kevin Bales, *Disposable People: New Slavery in the Global Economy* (Berkeley: University of California Press, 2004); Heather M. Smith "Sex Trafficking: Trends, Challenges, and the Limitations of International Law." *Human Rights Review* 12.3 (2011): 271–286. See also "Human Trafficking," Wikipedia, last modified August 24, 2014. Available online: https://en.wikipedia.org/wiki/Human_trafficking#India_Anti_Human_Trafficking_Portal

The Indian government considers all kinds of human trafficking (commercial sexual exploitation, forced labor, forced marriages, and domestic servitude) an organized crime. The Indian Penal Code "provides stringent punishment for human trafficking; trafficking of children for exploitation in any form including physical exploitation; or any form of sexual exploitation, slavery, servitude or the forced removal of organs."[43]

Imagine ... "removal of organs" ... Pretty sick.

What leadership by example looks like
Okay, so what happens if you run into victims of this sad and evil trade? That question was answered by one of the graduates of Peoples Baptist Bible College and Seminary. He is a pastor who, for his own safety, must remain nameless.

He along with several other pastors organized a way to help some of these girls at the risk of their own lives. Some have been sold by their relatives. They've been beaten up, sexually abused, and used as child labor, among other things. It's devastating.

This pastor saw the need and was willing to go and rescue them. He came to Brother G.S. and asked, "Will you help me." Without having to think about it a second time, G.S. said, "If you will rescue them, I will help you."

The girl's home in Dehradun, Uttarakhand State, is a place of safety and refuge.

---

43   "Human Trafficking."

But where and how would the funds be provided? Exactly where and how they were provided for George Müller—through praying and trusting the Lord to provide.

And so Peoples Baptist Ministries to India, through this pastor, has established a home for some of these abused girls. It's called Peoples Baptist Girls Home. Twenty-five girls live there now.

This pastor, his wife, and the local church are caring for these twenty-five young girls, but they do it in a rented building. The needs are ongoing. The rent has to be paid, and food and clothing has to be supplied for these victims.

But isn't that what Christians are supposed to do? How else can you demonstrate to these young girls that our God is a father of the fatherless?

> *A father of the fatherless, and a judge of the widows, is God in his holy habitation. (Psalm 68:5)*

Now this home is not here simply for the humanitarian work alone, although that by itself is indeed worthy.

The home is here to show these young girls the love of Christ and lead them to a saving knowledge of him. And many of these girls have come to know our Lord and Savior Jesus Christ. But isn't that the whole point?

Isn't that why we are here?

The goal ultimately is to build a home for them. But all of this takes a sizable investment. And it's up to God's people to figure out how they can meet this need.

If you were doing this type of work, wouldn't you want to expand and find more of these kids and be able to replicate the program? Now you can understand the conundrum of Peoples Baptist Ministries to India. There's a never-ending need for resources to meet the needs of the people.

What's noteworthy is that this girl's home wasn't G.S.'s idea; it was the anonymous pastor's idea. But here's the thing; a true leader is one who inspires others to do great things. And then helps whenever he or she can. It's what an entrepreneurial Christian does. It's what G.S. Nair does.

And that's what this team of two entrepreneurial Christians (G.S. and the pastor) did. They saw a problem and solved it by meeting the need.

The great thing, as far as we're concerned, is that there already exists in India those who have the desire and the leadership capability to do the work of the ministry. All they need is our help.

A Ladies' Home

Under the auspices of Penuel Baptist Church, housing is provided for poor, mostly widowed ladies who need care. And sadly, while some of these have family who could help them, they've been rejected by those families because of their faith in the Lord Jesus Christ.

There's also a...

Ministry to Lepers

People with leprosy are usually unemployable and, worse, they are rejected by their families even after they are cured.

They end up living in government-provided leper rehabilitation centers. But it's not like you think. All the government does is provide them with shelter. It's up to them to go beg for food.

*Feeding men and women at the leprosy colony in Haldwani,
Uttarakhand State*

PBMI has ministries at two centers, one in the city of Raipur in
Chhattisgarh State (in the central part of India) and another in the
city of Haldwani in Uttarakhand State in the far north. Pastor Ravi
Malachi and Pastor Sikpka are ministering in these places.

They have a gospel outreach to these folks and some have come to
know the Lord Jesus Christ as their Savior. Rather than have them
beg, the ministry tries to provide at least two or three meals weekly
as well as clothing.

Some of these folks have children, but they are not allowed to stay
with their parents. So PBMI has a couple of children's homes near
the two leper centers where they care for most of their children.

Although the government provides a clinic, sometimes they have to
go and buy their own medications, so PBMI tries to help with this as
well. Both areas can get very cold (35°F) and very hot (over 120°F)
so in addition to food, clothing, and medication, blankets and fans
are also supplied.

Assisted Living Home

There is a home for elderly believers (ages 65 and up), both men and women, most of whom have been abandoned by their families and thrown out of their homes because of their faith in the Lord Jesus Christ. These are folks who are unable to work and are taken care of by a local church.

Residents gather on the porch for the dedication of the old age home in Trivandrum District, Kerala State.

Persecution and Disaster Relief

Christians are a small minority in India, and there are times when our brothers and sisters are persecuted for their faith. They've been threatened, frightened, beaten, had their property burned or stolen, yet they persevere. It's our duty to respond to their needs, and PBMI does.

Disasters are also part of life in India. Aid doesn't come as fast as in other parts of the world, especially in the United States. When brothers and sisters in Christ are suffering, PBMI does all it can to help them—whether the cause is flooding, typhoon, earthquake, tsunami, or other types of natural disasters.

Not only does PBMI help those who are in need, it makes sure to give them the gospel at the same time.

Delivering rice to earthquake victims in Nepal

Medical and Drug Rehabilitation Center

PBMI is currently praying that the Lord would provide land and property so it can establish a drug rehabilitation and medical center. This is a large project that would cost in the area of $750,000. God willing, the plan is to open the center by 2018.

PART 4

Ministry-building secrets of G.S. Nair revealed

CHAPTER 10

Prayer that gets results from God

Can we find a friend so faithful who will all our sorrows share?
Jesus knows our every weakness; take it to the Lord in prayer.[44]

George Müller (1805–1898) was a Christian evangelist and director of the Ashley Down orphanage in Bristol, England, where he cared for over 10,000 orphans during his lifetime. His five orphanages cost over £100,000 to build, but Müller did it without going into debt and without ever asking for financial support. Rather, "Müller prayed about everything and expected each prayer to be answered."[45]

Similarly, G.S. prays about everything and expects each prayer to be answered.

> *Ask, and it shall be given you; seek, and ye shall find;*
> *knock, and it shall be opened unto you: (Matthew 7:7)*

Müller had five principles of prayer that gets results from God. I wasn't surprised to find that a look at some of G.S.'s sayings and comments on prayer matched up with Müller's principles.[46]

---

44   Joseph M. Scriven, "What a Friend We Have in Jesus" (1855). Scriven wrote this poem to comfort his mother in Ireland while he was living in Canada. Charles Crozat Converse composed the tune that made it a beloved hymn in 1868. Available online: https://en.wikipedia.org/wiki/What_a_Friend_We_Have_in_Jesus

45   "George Müller," Wikipedia, last modified July 25, 2015. Available online: https://en.wikipedia.org/wiki/George_M%C3%BCller

46   Arthur Tappan Pierson, *George Müller of Bristol* (London: James Nisbet, 1899), p. 170. Available online: https://play.google.com/store/books/details/Arthur_Tappan_Pierson_George_M%C3%BCller_of_Bristol?id=EFbkOf1YoJQC

Prayer Principles	Müller	Nair
Basis	"The first lays the basis of all prayer, in our oneness with the great High Priest." (You must be a born-again Christian.)	Christ should be the heart of your life.
Purity	"The second states a condition of prayer, found in the abandonment of sin."	There is no pillow so soft as a clear conscience.
Belief	"The third reminds us of the need of honoring God by faith that He is, and is the Rewarder of the diligent seeker."	You cannot do the Lord's ministry in man's power.
God's Glory	"The fourth reveals the sympathy with God that helps us to ask what is for our good and His glory."	You should be a successful Christian, but your success is to glorify God.
Persistence	"The last teaches us that, having laid hold of God in prayer, we are to keep hold until His arm is outstretched in blessing."	Ask for the same things every day in prayer until he does it.

The eighteen-month prayer marathon

G.S. and the ministry undertook a huge building project in 2003–2004. It was the construction of a 74,000 square foot, four-story, 3,500-seat auditorium, classroom, and office facility.

Construction on the Bible college and seminary's auditorium

The ministry had never undertaken anything of this scope before.

The project demanded to be bathed in prayer. So they began a nonstop 24/7 prayer marathon that lasted—if you can believe it—eighteen months. One hundred forty-four people prayed every day in two-hour shifts.

What did they pray for? Safety for the more than three hundred plus laborers and, more importantly, the salvation of their souls.

Jehovah Shamma *("Jehovah is there") greets visitors to the auditorium/office facility, completed in 2005.*

And the results?

They were remarkable; sixty-seven of those workers came to know the Lord Jesus Christ as their own Savior. And the building was finished without any problems, mishaps, or accidents. Not only that, but the Lord provided every penny that was necessary to finish the building and equip it without any debt—an expenditure of over $1 million.

An interior view of the 3,500-seat auditorium

Whenever souls are being saved, you can expect opposition.

It was during this time that G.S. and his family were threatened and had to move to Bangalore. G.S. would come back to Trivandrum every other week to inspect and check up on the work. There was a good company of people working with G.S. on the management of the construction and in constant prayer.

The opposition to the building project was a minor thing compared to the salvation of the souls of those workers.

The take-away is that prayer is not easy. According to G.S., you should always expect opposition from the enemy. Prayer is a weapon. The enemy knows it. It bothers him. He doesn't roll over; he will oppose you even as you prevail in prayer seeking the Lord's will, his help, and his good pleasure.

Prayer and doubt

If you've ever started a business or headed up a major project, then you know what doubts feel like.

You doubt your abilities, your decisions, and your talents. You constantly question yourself and everyone around you. Should you have even started this venture in the first place? You conjure up a hundred meetings that you'll never actually have. And when the big meeting finally does take place, it never turns out the way you thought it would.

The missionary-entrepreneur of India has to deal with the same doubts we have. Here is his advice…

> Doubt is a kind of unbelief because you're not fully trusting. I remember when during our first project in buying land to build the Bible Institute we had persecution. We almost lost all our money and were unable to build on the property, so the only thing I could do was pray.
>
> I prayed for seven days with other friends.
>
> I could sit there and doubt if it's God's will or ask, "Why did I do that?" Double-mindedness always brings questions—a thousand questions and no real answers.
>
> Many times questions bring answers that don't come from faith. Because satisfying your doubts gets done with intellectualism—not faith.

The remedy for doubt

> So I just went to prayer. I think the remedy for doubt is prayer, trusting in him, and waiting with anticipation for his answer. If you quit praying, you will doubt—when you are doubting you are not trusting the Lord.

I said, "Lord, you gave the money. Now we have a problem. Did I make a mistake? Are you not in this? I know that you just open the opportunity. It's not my interest, it's yours. It's all for you. So Lord, I need a remedy for this situation."

Instead of doubting what I have done, I just turn the doubt into a matter of prayer to him and I claim victory. Yes, it is real! I know he hears and answers. Pray without ceasing. You are to just tell him what he has done in the past, praising him, trusting him, and hoping for what he's going to do in the future and in this situation.

It's not something you pray and then just finish. You continually pray. You pray without ceasing.

What does this mean?

I'm not repeating things like unbelieving Gentiles do. I'm just giving thanksgiving that he's going to work. He's going to do it. Like he tells us in his word:

Be careful for nothing; but in every thing by prayer and supplication with thanksgiving let your requests be made known unto God. (Philippians 4:6)

Suppose I need some funds? I pray every day. I ask for the same things every day until he does it. It's not that I'm repeating myself, but I'm just repeating my request to the Lord with faith and anticipation.

Sometimes the Lord delays so that we trust in him instead of trusting in our own prayers. (I.e., some say "I prayed and prayed and finally God answered." This is opposite of the truth. We must trust the Lord—not our prayer effort.

Paul prayed three times. The first time he did not get an answer, the second time he didn't get an answer, but the third time the answer came. But he did not stop praying over the matter. He just asked God to give him grace to suffer that thing. That is what prayer is. It's not one time or two times or three times; it's a hundred times ... you need to ask him and trust in him.

God promised Elijah that it would rain, yet he prayed for the promised rain seven times.[47]

If you need to pray and ask for something once, does that mean you don't have anything else to talk about? You have to say, "Lord, this is my need. Thank you for helping me in the past. I know you're able to do it." I'm just pleading and praising and putting my needs before him. How many times do you have to ask for revival? I've been through revivals a few times.

It's happened in my ministry at least once in Manipur and several times in Orissa, but I pray for revival every day. It's something that we ought to pray for continually. I pray for souls every day. I pray, "Lord, save many souls in India." Is that finished? No, I pray for individuals sometimes in various places.

So in every matter of your needs, you can just bring all these things before him asking him to work and graciously look upon that matter.

I prayed for my father and mother for sixteen years before they got saved.

Consider the book of Daniel. He was perplexed by a vision, and he prayed to God, but God answered in twenty-one days.[48] So sometimes the answer could be held up.

---

47 See I Kings 18.

48 See Daniel 10.

Why is that?

> I think most probably the Lord allows delays to build up our faith and remove our doubt. Or maybe God is challenging the devil, who just opposed him, to show him that his servant is praying continually and depending upon him. We do not know.

Our warfare is not carnal.

> There is a spiritual war that we continually fight every day. That's why we need to pray continually. It's not that you pray for one thing and ask him and then stop because there may be a hindrance.
>
> Suppose the Lord thinks that we should present the need we have to somebody else?
>
> Then we pray over that. If that person is not obedient to meet the needs, then you have to pray that God would open his heart and touch him. People can be disobedient, so we need to pray continually. It's not that we just ask one time and are finished.

Every religion under heaven teaches people to pray. But we pray because he has invited us to pray!

> *Call unto me, and I will answer thee, and shew thee great and mighty things, which thou knowest not. (Jeremiah 33:3)*

Healings in Jesus' name—more answers to prayer

G.S. tells of one pastor who had asked him to preach at Trinity Baptist Church in Trivandrum.

He was invited into one of the believer's homes where there was a small child about eight or ten years old. The parents were exhausted having brought their child for treatment after treatment and still he did not get well.

Then I took the boy and kept him on my lap and prayed. And that sickness never came back to him afterward. This boy literally got cured and ultimately became a pastor.

G.S. doesn't like to tell too much about these sorts of things because people focus on that. He says God answers many prayers in response to sickness. And he provides many needs and removes many hindrances in a tremendous way. He says he sees answers to prayers every day because there are so many needs in the ministry; he says it's all answers to prayer.

His parents and sister getting saved was a great answer to prayer.

In over forty years of ministry, thousands of answers to prayer have happened. Like the time the Lord provided petrol for us at 1:30 in the morning.

We were traveling in Orissa State and we ran out of diesel. It was around 11 o'clock at night. We were about fifty miles away from our destination. So we all began to pray and continued to pray. And then around 1:30 a.m. a truck came by. We stopped the truck and told the man that we had run out of diesel. He laughed at me. I said, "You are mocking us!"

He said, "No, no. The thing is that usually I stop in another town and stay there, but after eating food I could not sleep, so we decided to drive on. We went and filled our tank but there was an extra ten-liter can and I filled it. I had never done that before, and that's why I was laughing. I did not know that I was filling the tank for you."

Then he gave us that ten-liter can of fuel. So our answer to prayer came around 1:30 or 2:00 in the morning. For some things I have prayed for many years, and for other things the Lord answers the same day. But he always provides.

G.S. tells a story about his first transportation, which was a bicycle given to him by Miss Isabel Swanson.

> She was one of my prayer warriors from the beginning of the ministry. She was one of the missionaries from Baptist Mid-Missions in Assam, India.
>
> She eventually came to Bangalore and worked at Berean Baptist Bible College with Dr. Jacob Chelli when I was a student there. She treated me like I was her son. She used to come during my summer outreach ministry and travel with me.
>
> So one day I asked her to pray for a bicycle. She wrote a note saying, "I will pray for a bicycle for you." She wrote another note in a week's time and said, "I went to the auction and I was able to get a twelve-year-old bicycle for you."

That may seem to be a small thing to you, but if you are a budding missionary-entrepreneur with a burning desire to serve the Lord, this was a huge answer to prayer and a huge blessing from one of the dear saints of God.

G.S. Nair's biggest fear—legacy

As successful entrepreneurs get older, one of the things they are concerned about is their legacy. What is it that they have accomplished that can make the world a better place because they were here?

> My biggest fear is about those who we are raising up today; will they be strong in faith in the days to come? I see in the next generation a faith that is kind of shallow and watered down.
>
> Referring to the time of his second coming, the Lord asks this question:
>
> ... *Nevertheless when the Son of man cometh, shall he find faith on the earth? (Luke 18:8)*

The Christian walk is about more than just believing in him; it's about trusting and depending on him to meet our needs day by day.

So that's one of my great needs in prayer—for the younger generation, that they may grow stronger and stronger and stronger in faith looking unto the Savior and building a relationship with him.

For example, recently one of the churches supported a pastor and wanted the ministry to help in his support. But there are another ten pastors who didn't have enough support.

This man has a need, and he's always asking, asking, asking for help. He says, "I need to get more support." My letter to him was that "you trust in the Lord. You pray to him instead of asking for this thing. God can provide for that."

That is how I build up young people: They must trust in the Lord. Our ministry did not start by seeing the funds, our ministry started by seeing the power of God to meet the needs.

There are a lot of "hard" workers. But what we need are "faithful" workers.

CHAPTER 11

Q&A with Dr. Nair

Serving the Lord is an opportunity and privilege.
It's not like a burden. —G.S. Nair

What is the secret to establishing so many churches?

God has challenged our hearts: "I will build my church."
God is investing in and building his people. The church
is people saved by the grace of God, washed with the
precious blood of the Lord Jesus Christ, and added to
his body. That is God's plan for everyone, everywhere.

We see areas where there is no testimony for the Lord
Jesus Christ and it is the desire of God that people be
saved and churches established. But somebody is there
to stop it. Yes, the devil is trying. But the devil is not
going to stop it.

So we have to continually do the work as far as the end
of the earth. Our aim is to take the gospel not just to our
local area but to other areas as well.

Our pattern is fourfold:

1. Winning souls,

2. Discipling them by teaching,

3. Maturing them by establishing local churches and
   teaching them to observe the Word of God, and

4. Encouraging them to bring others to Christ.

As they bring other souls, the church multiplies.

My greatest soul winners are the church members. The sheep bring the lambs, not the shepherd [pastor], so we always encourage them, especially new believers, to just go and witness to other people, so that by discipling they do that work along with the pastors.

How does one balance ministry with family?

G.S. has four children and six grandchildren. He has a ministry that spans four countries. He's the president of three Bible Colleges and one seminary. Have you ever wondered how such a man could balance his family and his other responsibilities?

My children are grown up and gone. I am so thankful for my wife for taking care of my children properly and for being such a good wife and mother. If she didn't do these things, the ministry would not exist.

That's one of the reasons I really value women's ministry. They are so important. I always say that when God calls you, he is calling your wife and your whole family. You are not serving alone.

Whenever I could, I would go to my son's football (soccer) games, and I was involved in the lives of my three girls whenever I could as well. If I couldn't make it to a game, my wife or his sisters would go. But always somebody representing the family was there.

My children knew that I was in the ministry. I'm not somewhere else. They respected that. And they still do. I also told my wife and children that if you folks aren't walking with the Lord that will be the end of me serving as well, because we are also serving the Lord as a family. If my family fails I count that as a failure for me. I am serving and they are supporting me. But we are serving each other and we are laborers together.

God has given me good health, a good wife, and good children so that I might be able to serve the Lord in a better way. The blessings of God should not be a burden or hindrance for the ministry.

I try to impress this upon the pastors also. If you cannot take care of your wife, if you cannot live peacefully as a family, you should not be serving the Lord in full-time ministry.

If the ministry is first, the family must also be first. God gives you a good wife, good children, and good family for the betterment of the ministry. You add value to the ministry by living in a good and close fellowship with your family.

Does that leave room for hobbies?

Some days, my hobby is coming home and getting to chat with my children or just play with them.

I like to garden. I do gardening at the college sometimes. I like cooking, and I sometimes cook at the college too.

G.S. cooking at the college in Trivandrum

Besides reading the Scriptures, I also read things mostly related with the ministry as well as any good publication that gives some insight for helping the ministry.

Plus, I write for The Baptist Voice, which is a ministry publication published once a month. We hope to put it online soon.

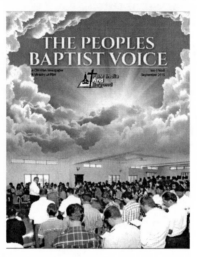

The Peoples Baptist Voice *is a monthly publication of PBMI.*

What are your favorite Bible verses?

I have many favorite verses. John 3:16 is a fantastic verse. But my **life verse** is:

Faithful is he that calleth you, who also will do it.
(1 Thessalonians 5:24)

Here are three more:

But they that wait upon the LORD shall renew their strength; they shall mount up with wings as eagles; they shall run, and not be weary; and they shall walk, and not faint. (Isaiah 40:31)

A Psalm of David. Fret not thyself because of evildoers, neither be thou envious against the workers of iniquity. For they shall soon be cut down like the grass, and wither as the green herb. Trust in the Lord, and do good; so shalt thou dwell in the land, and verily thou shalt be fed. Delight thyself also in the Lord; and he shall give thee the desires of thine heart. Commit thy way unto the Lord; trust also in him; and he shall bring it to pass. And he shall bring forth thy righteousness as the light, and thy judgment as the noonday. Rest in the Lord, and wait patiently for him: fret not thyself because of him who prospereth in his way, because of the man who bringeth wicked devices to pass. (Psalm 37:1-7)

Have not I commanded thee? Be strong and of a good courage; be not afraid, neither be thou dismayed: for the Lord thy God is with thee whithersoever thou goest.

(Joshua 1:9)

What books have given you the most practical knowledge?

I've learned the most practical knowledge from reading, learning, and teaching the book of Romans.

As far as authors are concerned, I really like books by Oswald Sanders and John Phillips and a few others.

I was challenged by author A. W. Tozer and especially his books The Pursuit of God and The *Knowledge of the Holy*: The Attributes of God, Their Meaning in the Christian Life.

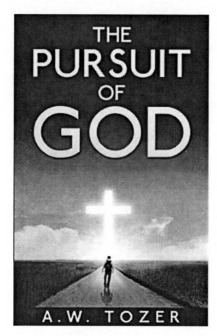

First published in 1948, The Pursuit of God *by A.W. Tozer has inspired many believers through the years.*

I once met Homer Duncan while I was a student in Bible College and felt the presence of God as he was praying. He wrote a book titled Revival Fires. One of the stories was about the revival under Evan Roberts in Wales. I was challenged by the great work of the Lord under Roberts.

Another book that greatly influenced me is Why Revival Tarries by Leonard Ravenhill.

Who are your heroes apart from the Bible?

My heroes apart from the Bible or men I respect are Dr. Alan T. Ironside (cousin of H. A. Ironside), who was my Bible school professor, and Dr. Jacob Chelli, who was president of Berean Baptist Bible College and Seminary.

But then there are the servants of the Lord who have faithfully stood by me and promoted the Lord's ministry in India by prayer and practical support for many years:

Dr. Dudley and Carol Long from Albany, NY, and Mel and Donna Moody from Dublin Christian Academy in Dublin, NH, who introduced me to churches in the United States; and Don and Sally Chisholm of Osterville, MA, who have done so much for the ministry over the last twenty years.

And others like:

Pastor Jeff and Karen Amsbaugh of Johnston, RI; Barry and Bonnie Blenis of Albany, NY; Pastor Bob and Barbara Hanson of Plymouth, MA; Pastor Stewart and Sue Hunt of Damascus, PA; Ms. Carol Kierstead of Greenville, SC; Dr. Bill and Brenda Kennedy, Glasgow, Scotland; Jack and Susan McElroy of Groton, MA; Pastor Joe and Pat Pagano of Middletown, PA; Pastor Barry and Bette Somerville of Geneva, NY; Ms. Margaret Welch of Albany, NY; Dr. Brian and Fleur Whenham of Condell Park, Australia; and, of course, my wonderful family.

How do you avoid burnout in the ministry?

I never knew that you could get burned out. I mean, I know it happens to a lot of guys, but I think it's from trusting themselves, working in their own knowledge and effort, and not looking unto God. In a sense, Elijah was burned out when he ran off because the previous day he was doing something great.

You have to see the ministry as God's ministry—not yours. If you see it as yours, you will lose it.

Often times it happens that people won't promote young people because they are afraid of losing "their" ministry. We are really just caretakers. God can use others instead of us, but we should be thankful that he is using us for the time being.

God saved David one day, and the next day David said he was going to die and was sick of life. I strongly believe that we have to focus upon the Lord. Sometimes self-pity is one of the things that makes you burn out.

How do you define success?

In the ministry success is not how much you've done or how many souls you have won. The fruit comes from the Lord, but success is determined by how faithfully you keep sowing the seed. Success is not how much you harvest, but how faithfully you sow the seed every day.

Why do you face constant financial burdens?

The pressure of the ministry is to meet the mountain of needs. My good friend Margaret Welch once said that the needs of the ministry are bottomless, and it's true. That's because there is no bottom to the work. That's why we are working continually.

We're not satisfied doing some small work in a corner. No. The need in India and neighboring countries is great. We are ministering to almost one-fifth of the world's population. India alone contains 20 percent of the world's population.

So how can we stop? We can never stop.

When you think about the ministry, you're not talking about what "a" church is doing but what over 2,700 churches are doing. And what tens of thousands of people are doing, and what six hundred plus students are doing. That's a lot of stuff going on. Our ministry is so much broader than most people think.

Why do the colleges and seminary never advertise?

Almost all colleges advertise. We did do it once because of somebody's influence, but the motivation was not right. I have always opposed it because why should we crave students?

We do not need to crave students to sustain the ministry.

The students come to us because they are motivated to the cause by the caliber of our graduates and pastors. They want to be a part of the ministry because they see how someone else can be so excited and fulfilled about serving God.

"The students come to us because they are motivated to the cause..."

How do you motivate faculty and staff?

That's a good question, and it's a matter of prayer for me also.

If you don't have vision, people perish. If our faculty and staff don't have a vision for reaching out to people and doing it the Lord's way, then we will kill our own ministry.

I always say that if you don't have vision, you're committing suicide. You're not giving life; you're taking the life away.

So I always try to motivate our faculty, staff, pastors, and students by telling them that they need to have a vision and that the vision must always be in front of them.

Where there is no vision, the people perish...
(Proverbs 29:18)

What's the vision? The vision is to see the country like the Lord sees it. When Jesus saw the multitude coming, he saw that they were sheep without a shepherd. The vision he was transmitting to his disciples was that they should pray, therefore, to the Lord of the harvest that he may send forth more laborers.

The vision God gave me is to reach out and build His ministry, and I always try to transmit that vision to my people. And I pray the Holy Ghost to rekindle that vision in the faculty, staff, and students.

What makes for a true Christian leader?

I think it's a wonderful thing to think about being a leader. Everybody wants to be leader, but if you are not a follower, you cannot be a leader.

(The phrase "follow me" appears seventeen times in the Gospels.)

I strongly believe in servant leadership. You must serve so that you'll be able to motivate others to serve other people. Servant leadership—that's what we need.

For even the Son of man came not to be ministered unto,
but to minister, and to give his life a ransom for many.
(Mark 10:45)

So many times people think of a leader in terms of a position. It's not really a position. It's a matter of being a tool in the hand of God; being used by God. Then as God begins to use you, and people begin to see that you follow him, then people will start following you. That's how you become a leader.

The Lord said, "Follow me, and I will make you fishers of men."[49] In other words, if you don't follow me, you're not going to be a fisher of men. No following, no fishing, no leadership.

Without following the Lord, you cannot guide others. If you are not following, you cannot lead. So a good follower makes a good leader.

Like the Apostle Paul said:

Be ye followers of me, even as I also am of Christ. (1 Corinthians 11:1)

How do you make every minute count?

Every day is a good day, every day is a gift of God, and God expects us to work because he himself said:

I must work the works of him that sent me, while it is day: the night cometh, when no man can work. (John 9:4)

Jesus was reminding his disciples that they will not be able to work when the night comes.

And he said while there is a day, you can work. When there is an opportunity, you can work. So I often say, "Make every opportunity as a pulpit to exhibit the Lord Jesus Christ."

(Remember earlier how we saw that entrepreneurs are opportunity seekers?)

---

49   Matthew 4:19

Every opportunity is a God-given opportunity for you; you're here for only a time. No wonder Psalm 90:12 says:

So teach us to number our days, that we may apply our hearts unto wisdom.

Every day is a gift of God. Every minute is a gift of God, so we work continually.

Often I say, "We have to live every day, every hour, every minute in relationship with eternity because we are saved to eternity." We are accountable for eternity, and one day there will reveal what we have done during our short time here.

That does not mean I'm perfect. No, I've got failures; I've got infirmities. And when my focus changes, even I can go away, so we have to be careful.

How do you deal with stress?

Stress is part and parcel of ministry. The Lord understands the stress of the ministry. But stress itself is not the problem. It's all in how you look at it. Serving the Lord is an opportunity and privilege. It's not like a burden. When you see serving the Lord as a burden, it becomes stress for you.

There are lots of needs. Lots of decisions you have to make. It's not easy. But being under stress is not going to solve any problems. So I have to give it to somebody else.

The Lord is the most important person who can take my stress. So, sometimes I just walk away from the problem, maybe go and cook something, or maybe I just start singing knowing that my God will take over my problems and stress.

It's not easy to sing, but worry is not going to help you.

Just give it to him, and his unusual help will come sometime. He's working. He's able to do it. I know it's so hard sometimes when you see the need in front of you.

There hath no temptation taken you but such as is common to man: but God is faithful, who will not suffer you to be tempted above that ye are able; but will with the temptation also make a way to escape, that ye may be able to bear it. (1 Corinthians 10:13)

You really don't know what's going to happen. You may be just thinking about your own plan, programs, and all kind of things. You think, "This is not going to work," but then the answer comes, sometimes in marvelous ways.

As you learn to depend upon the Lord and trust in him, then you will able to deal with stress.

There is no formula anyone ever found to get over the stress of the ministry.

The Scripture says:

Be careful for nothing; but in every thing by prayer and supplication with thanksgiving let your requests be made known unto God.
(Philippians 4:6)

The thing we need to do is commit our ways to the Lord.

Psalm 37:5 says:

Commit thy way unto the LORD; trust also in him; and he shall bring it to pass.

And 1 Peter 5:7 says:
Casting all your care upon him; for he careth for you.

The important thing is you will come across burdens. You will come across care. You will come across stress. At the same time, this should motivate you to think about how Christ is concerned about you and your stress, and he is more than willing to help you with it.

You can give it to him but sometimes because you are human it's not easy. Once we start to learn how to hand our burdens and stress over to him, the easier it gets. We hand over these things to him simply by coming to him.

It's not easy because your mind and thoughts keep focusing on the problem. You have to try and close out your thoughts, otherwise it's not going to work. You need to think about the Lord Jesus instead of thinking about your problems. Think about him and talk to him like you talk to our Father.

Like as a father pitieth his children, so the LORD pitieth them that fear him. (Psalm 103:13)

So let's review…

Number one, you get a problem. So then you cast it onto the person who's caring for you.

At the same time, Philippians 4:6 says:

Be careful for nothing…

I always say, "Be careful for nothing?" Only people with a mental disease can say that and then just walk away!

But the Lord tells us WHAT to do with the care.

He tells us to "pray with thanksgiving."

Be careful for nothing; but in every thing by prayer and supplication **with thanksgiving** *let your requests be made known unto God.*

(Philippians 4:6)

That's like a bird with two wings. You're just praying with thanksgiving, and it flies to the Savior, so your burden will be lifted up as you hand it over to Him. Totally depend upon him.

And he gives you peace which passeth all understanding.

I do not know how, but I know he hears me and he gives me peace. There have been times of struggles in my life—oppositions, financial stress, financial needs, sometimes no doors are opening—but the only thing I do is cling to his promises and pray and God unusually works in somebody's heart and provides for my needs.

So, those are the things that motivate you.

Always, when stress comes, I think about God's past help in my life. The one who helped me is still alive and is willing to do it, and he never says "I cannot do it."

He'll never say that you're on your own. He'll never say that his resources have run out. His resources never run out.

Sometimes people say, "Sorry, I cannot give to your need." I've had friends who've given a lot in the past but are sometimes unable to help. But the thing is our Father is greater than these, and he can raise up means of support that we don't know about. I depend on that.

CHAPTER 12

Day-to-day operational challenges

> When you have a problem, don't worry about the
> greatness of the problem, but relax in the greatness
> of God. —G.S. Nair

Christian negotiation

If there's one thing about entrepreneurs, it's that they are usually very effective negotiators. But not the way people usually think. They recognize that in order for a deal to be successful, both sides have to be satisfied.

What's interesting about G.S. is that he does not negotiate with unbelievers when it comes to the ministry. Sound odd?

Somebody might say that he is not a wise steward of God's resources, especially considering the fact that in nearly forty years he has invested literally millions of dollars donated by God's people for buildings, transportation, and supplies.

You'd think that unless you knew the type of Lord's servant Brother G.S. is.

Here's what he said regarding negotiations with unbelievers.

> I don't negotiate with unbelieving people on ministry projects.
>
> There is a risk that they may think, "I'm doing a favor to God. Maybe God will favor me. Because of that, he will give me salvation."
>
> You never want to put a false trust on their hearts because people are willing to do something for God

in exchange for what they will get from him. They may think they are working out their karma by assisting in the Christian God's project.

So here is what I say, "This is for the ministry. I'm not making any profit. So make enough profit for yourself but not too much."

So they think about that.

Sometimes people say that when you see some property, you should just pray to God that he would give it to you. God doesn't do that. Although he may do that sometimes, he is not going to just loot somebody else, even unbelievers, and give it to you.

I see many people say that you are supposed to "name it and claim it." Maybe they should say name it and claim it and stole it! If you don't pay, you end up in jail. Sometimes that attitude can lead to overconfidence.

My God has provided always. I often say this is a faith ministry.

How we get along with opposing neighbors

We always try as much as we can to live peacefully with other people no matter what religion they are. You should never provoke people. Try to be a witness to them instead of a troublemaker for them.

Sometimes Christians are high-minded and look down on everybody else like they're dirt. You're not going to bring anyone to the Lord that way.

We have to see the value of their souls rather than how they act and how they're in sin. The problem with us is that sometimes we calculate their sinful life and we don't think about the value of their soul to Jesus Christ, who died for them.

We try to, just as much as we can, exhibit the Lord Jesus Christ to them. They might be able to see that we are concerned for them. That's the way we can connect with them.

The challenge of meeting a payroll

Every entrepreneur knows this pressure well. Everybody else gets paid FIRST—especially staff. Here are G.S.' comments…

I often remind the staff that this is a faith ministry as well. Sometimes they forget that. Every first week of the month comes around and they need their salary.

But sometimes it can be delayed. So I say, "You've worked with me for so many years. Do I owe you anything? It may not have been paid the first week, but the second. But you surely got it. And when it comes to their salary, we try to give them a raise of around 10 percent every year because they are in such need.

I don't want to see Christian workers remain poor always. At the same time, they should not have a lavish lifestyle, and that's why we try to give a raise of around 10 percent every year. But sometimes there's not enough. But they know that if we have it, we'll give it.

Sometimes people ask about our budget. We do create budgets, but if the funds don't come in, what do you do with your budget?

I often remind the staff that you get your salary, we thank God, and you go away happy. But the next moment I'm thinking about how I'm going to pay next month. So I tell them to please pray that God would provide.

I tell them, "Maybe God is using this institution. We did not call you. God called you and he's the one faithfully providing for you, so keep on asking Him and trusting him instead of the institution to provide for your needs."

How to instill a right kind of spirit in staff and students

I always tell people that our ministry is like a family. It's not only G.S. Nair's family; we all are part and parcel of God's family. God brought us together to work together.

If you cannot cooperate, we are not pressuring you or pleading with you to stay here. If you don't want to stay, you may just walk away. But if you want to stay, you must be a person bringing unity as a family here.

We work together as a family. This is not G.S. Nair's ministry. It is not somebody's ministry. It is the ministry of God, and when you are part and parcel of that ministry you are serving the Lord, not individuals.

Sadly, some become leaders and talk about things like it's "their" ministry.

I have never called this "my" ministry. I have always called it "our" ministry. Never, ever, even in chapel, in our church, or to the staff, have I ever claimed this to be "my" ministry. I always say "our" ministry. I am very careful with that. Because truly it is the Lord's ministry.

Of course, without staff we cannot do the work. God has given us these men and women so we have to treat them like our brothers and sisters and work together.

How to hire the best workers

If anybody comes to our ministry asking for a job, we never take them. This is not a job. It's a way to serve the Lord. Secondly, if people ask, "How much can you give me?" we never take them simply because we are not sure how much we are able to give.

Jesus Christ said, I will meet your needs. That does not mean you should always live poor and be begging, but I always say that God is calling and he is able to provide. He will never call us if he cannot provide for us.

If they say they are willing to serve with this institution and they have a family, then surely we know that and we will try to help as much as we can, but I tell them that they must try to live with what the Lord provides. But if we have more, then we will give. As time goes on, we just see the needs—their children, their schooling, and their environment of renting; we take all those things into account, and then we prayerfully decide.

How to dismiss someone the right way

We've had to let a few of our staff members go. Not because of salary, but because of different principles. For example:

One time we had a faculty member who went to another college for an interview while he was teaching in our college without our knowledge.

First of all, he told us he was going to meet with friends so we wouldn't know. Instead, he went on the interview. Now doctrinally this other college does not agree with us. And yet he is working with us and is considering working for them.

So a few people came to know about his interview and that he was hiding it from the leadership.

I came and asked him about it and said, "Brother, I heard you went to meet your family." He said, "Yes." I hadn't ask him that before, and I didn't want to make him lie to me, so I just said, "Did you go to that college? Did you go for an interview?"

He said, "Yes." I said, "You are here at this college and you know that they teach other doctrines. How can you go there?"

So I said, "We will give you three or four months' salary for this year, but you don't work for us anymore. You're free from today."

He was surprised at how I found out. At the same time, I was concerned about him, so we gave him a salary for three or four months so he wouldn't starve. I couldn't keep him here because of the risk that he would teach wrong doctrine to our students and because of the inconsistency of his faith. Even still, he went away as a brother and friend. I know he respected me. But sometimes people can turn against you also.

How we determine which students to admit to the college

First of all, we go to their pastors and find out their character. I am looking for a born-again, called-of-God-for-service person. I am not just looking for people to fill our classrooms. Sometimes people have the wrong motives.

They may not have been accepted somewhere else for secular studies and sometimes want to come here.

If they're not willing to serve the Lord because they don't feel the call of God, even though they want to come here, we don't take those kinds of people. We want to see that people are willing to serve so we communicate with their pastors and people in the church and try to find out about their motivation.

We don't always get it 100 percent right, but we quickly realize before too long the need to deal with them to correct their motives or let them go.

That's the most important. With regard to tuition, we ask them how much they can pay. Some can pay maybe $2, some $4 or $5 or $20 per month for tuition, room, and board. Our actual cost per month per student for tuition, room, and board is $95 per month.

We provide our education tuition-free to worthy candidates if they are poor and unable to pay if they are really called of God.

How we train for women's ministry

We always want women to be involved in the church.

Before they come to the college, we make sure they are interested in serving the Lord and not just to have some English education or even to find a husband. But it's not as if relationships have not developed—maybe around 5 percent have met their spouse at college.

But we always encourage them to just focus on their studies. We tell them that the God who saved you is able to give you the right person at the right time. Don't just go because of what you are seeing.

Lady graduates with the Nairs in Trivandrum

I jokingly tell the girls, "Don't trust any of our boys. They are demons." And I tell the boys, "Don't trust any of the girls because they are fallen angels."

If we come across some kind of evil appearance, we try to deal with them carefully and talk to them and bring them out from that.

The thing is that, no way they can disregard the discipline of the college. We are building up character. That's the reason I don't like online courses. I want the students to stay at the campus because it's through human interaction that their character can be shaped according to his desire.

"Building character is one of the most important things we do."

Character can't be shaped online.

Anybody can do an online course from their home. I think this is one of the great mistakes of online courses especially for people who are endeavoring to serve the Lord.

It's not the same as a secular business. Part of why we are here is to shape their character because we are dealing with souls and eternity. If you bring the wrong person to pastor your church who has an online course even with a doctoral degree, if they don't have a good and godly character, they can ruin the people.

Maybe many people will not agree with me. But I strongly believe that Jesus is for character development. Why else would he stay with his disciples three-and-a-half years? He obviously did it to develop their character.

They were from miserable communities. They were fishermen. They weren't even good at languages. They had no skills other than fishing. Some were tax collectors. Jesus lived with them; he taught them; he rebuked them and made them learn. And that's what I want.

We need to have the right kind of life on the campus. How will they be after four or five years? A degree on a piece of paper is of no use if they can't win souls and disciple others.

We have to build up their life; build up their character. As Jesus was going to be crucified, everybody abandoned him. But the Holy Spirit came upon the disciples and brought all things to their remembrance that the Lord had taught them. Which is why people said, "They had been with Jesus."[50]

These people recognized that the disciples acted like Jesus and spoke like Jesus. That is character, and that is what is needed in today's Christian workers.

---

50   Acts 4:13

CHAPTER 13

How the missionary-entrepreneur added some "self-funding" to the ministry

*Cast thy bread upon the waters: for thou shalt find it
after many days. (Ecclesiastes 11:1)*

Here's the story of how some like-minded entrepreneurs got together with G.S. and figured out how to make the ministry partially self-funding.

> We are in a country where Christianity is very much in the minority. Although they allow us to exist today, we don't know what the future will bring because not only has the government put out foreign missionaries, there is also a tendency toward nationalism here.
>
> They may stop all foreign funds. This is why I thought about having some "self-income." But at the same time, we don't want to have too much so that future generations can just live off of that. It must be strictly for the ministry.
>
> Plus, I was looking for some jobs that we can provide for the students and maybe for some pastors.

Rubber plantations

G.S. presented the idea to some like-minded entrepreneurs, and they invested money in some rubber plantations and a small dairy farm.

> So we have ten acres of rubber trees from which we get some income, although I would like to get around twenty-five acres in different locations, possibly in Tamil Nadu State. Also, I would like to

get wheat and paddy fields and a good dairy farm in Punjab.

We have two acres of fruit and vegetables, coconuts, most of which we use in the college.

We also plant black pepper and get about seventy kilos per year, some of which we can sell. I would like to get about ten acres in the Tea Plantation area. Things grow very well there.

We have dairy cows, and we get milk from them and methane from their dung for cooking fuel.

Livestock are raised at the college help support the ministry.

A medical clinic and other possibilities

We are looking to establish a clinic with a drug rehabilitation center. The facility would create some income, but we would supply our services at a discounted rate and use it as a means of evangelism.

In the future, I'd like to have a technical school and computer training center to give some other skills to our students so they can be self-sufficient.

CHAPTER 14

Two reasons to invest in PBM India

God is no man's debtor. —G.S. Nair

If you like challenges, this is a worthy one.

India is the second largest mission field on earth. And this field is white unto harvest. Only China is bigger; however, according to a United Nations study, India is set to overtake China as the world's most populous country by 2022.[51]

But India has been a closed mission field since 1978, which means India can only be reached by native missionaries.

And, as the Lord would have it, this turns out to be the most efficient and cost-effective way to reach any people group.

Here are two reasons to invest in PBM India:

1. The man—G.S. Nair

- He's not just a "church planter," but he has created a system to produce "church-planting pastors."
- He's not just a "pastor-teacher," but he's an educator who develops "pastor-teachers."
- He's not just a soul winner, but he's a soul-winning leader who teaches others how to win souls.
- He's not just a "humanitarian," but he's an "evangelical humanitarian leader" who has created a charitable organization that actually does and says everything we say we believe in.

---

51   Emma Batha, "India Set to Overtake China as World's Most Populous Country by 2022: UN," July 30, 2015. Available online: http://www.interaksyon.com/article/115117/india-set-to-overtake-china-as-worlds-most-populous-country-by-2022-un (accessed August 19, 2015).

2. The mission the man built—Peoples Baptist Ministries to India (PBMI)

PBM India is a life-changing, dynamic, and proven ministry that is run and controlled by one local church, Peoples Baptist Church of Trivandrum, Kerala State, India. G.S. Nair is the founder and pastor of this church.

Following the Lord Jesus Christ and under the leadership of the Holy Spirit, Dr. G.S. Nair and his team have been fulfilling the Great Commission since 1976. The burden of seeing millions going to hell and the compassion of our Savior motivated them to forsake all and give their lives for the cause of Christ.

In 1976, after graduating from Bible College, G.S. Nair and three other students with only $5 and the leadership of the Holy Spirit went out to hold open-air meetings, give testimonies, hand out tracts, conduct Bible studies, and do personal discipleship; a work that ultimately led to the establishment of new churches.

They called their group Kerala Baptist Gospel Team. Kerala is the name of the state where they started.

A Proven, Repeatable, and Sustainable Model

Their success in soul winning, church planting, and disciple making stems from their use of a proven model that's repeatable and sustainable from one generation to the next.

And that model is their summer evangelistic church planting ministry…

Instead of going home for summer break, many of the students and faculty from the Bible colleges volunteer to become part of evangelistic teams that spread out all over India. A summer ministry can cover as many as fifteen states.

A crowd listens as G.S. shares God's word at an evangelistic meeting.

They typically send out at least thirty teams. Each consists of about 11 students and one faculty member. Here's what they do:

- Invite people to gospel meetings through door-to-door evangelism.

- Hand out hundreds of thousands of tracts per summer.

- Hold open-air meetings, leading to cottage meetings and Bible studies.

- Preach, sing, and give testimonies at evangelistic meetings.

- Deal one-on-one with inquirers, seeking to lead them to Christ.

- Do follow-up work, which results in Bible studies, baptism of new converts, establishing new churches and motivating them to reach their communities with the Gospel.

Through this method, more than 2,700 churches consisting of over 250,000 members have been established since 1976.

PBMI has been using this same proven method of evangelism, discipleship, and church planting for nearly forty years.

In 1980, as a ministry of Peoples Baptist Church, G.S. founded Peoples Baptist Bible College and Seminary (PBBC&S)[52] in order to train nationals to establish local Baptist churches throughout India and beyond.

The mission is threefold:
1. Win souls to Christ.
2. Establish local churches.
3. Disciple the new converts for further evangelism.

Since 1980 they've graduated over 3,200 church-planting pastors leading over 2,700 churches with over 250,000 members. Their success rate for putting pastors on the field over the past thirty-five years is over 80 percent.

It's your money and you should invest it wherever you feel you'll get the best return.

The Lord has entrusted to each of us a certain amount of resources. They are all within our power to use and invest how we see fit.

But one thing is for sure, the Lord loves a cheerful giver.

By investing in PBMI you have the opportunity to change the world—one soul at a time—by investing in a ministry with a thirty-nine-year track record of results using a proven, repeatable, and sustainable model.

---

52   See Peoples Baptist Bible College and Seminary website, http://www.pbbcs.org/

Plus, you are investing in the lives of:

1. A leadership team that is fervent about soul winning and church planting.

2. Pastors who've put their lives on the line to preach the gospel.

3. Students that have been carefully selected because of their commitment to the gospel of Jesus Christ.

4. Widows who are often rejected by family because of their faith in Christ.

5. The fatherless who need to learn of their Heavenly Father's love.

6. Lepers who are treated as outcasts.

7. Persecution and disaster victims who need to see the love of Christ.

The payoff for your investment?

All you'll need to hear are these words from our wonderful Savior, "Well done, *thou* good and faithful servant."

Join with Dr. G.S. Nair and Peoples Baptist Ministries to India and Beyond today!

Here's how you can have a part in the ministry:

To schedule Dr. Nair to speak at your church, please contact:

> Mr. Don Chisholm
> 137 Scudder Rd.
> Osterville, MA 02655
> (508)428-6989
>
> **dchisholm29@gmail.com**

To financially support the ministry:

- ✓ To donate online, visit **www.gsnair.org**

- ✓ Checks should be made out and sent to:

> **Fundamental Baptist Mission to India**
> 137 Scudder Rd.
> Osterville, MA 02655

Fundamental Baptist Mission to India is a 501(c)(3) non-profit charitable organization. It operates entirely with volunteer staff. No salaries are paid.

APPENDICES

Endorsements of Dr. G.S. Nair from some who have visited the ministry in India...

"The good hand of God is evident everywhere I looked. You [Dr. Nair] love the people and they love you. Your sacrifice for them is abundantly evident everywhere, as is your genuine love for their souls. I doubt that anyone anywhere has started more churches, supported more pastors than you have, and you have never seemed to grow weary in well-doing. Your vision appears to be larger now than ever."

Dr. Bob Jones III, Chancellor   Bob Jones University
Greenville, SC

"I had never met a person who was so fervent about winning the people of his nation to Christ. His love for the Lord, servant's heart, and passion for the lost was compelling. It wasn't long before our church began to support the ministry of Fundamental Baptist Mission to India (FBMI). I can think of no better place to encourage with your prayers and support with your finances."

Rev. Barry Somerville, Pastor   Finger Lakes Baptist Church
Geneva, NY

"Dr. G.S. Nair manifests the fruit of the Spirit in his daily walk. He has reproduced himself thousands of times over as the graduates of his Bible College and extension schools have evangelistically infiltrated a nation that will soon become the most populous on the face of the earth. Though Dr. Nair has been used to establish children's homes, Bible colleges, and various other innovative evangelistic outreaches, the heartbeat of Peoples Baptist Ministries from day one has been church planting. Thousands of churches have already been planted, and yet there is no maintenance mentality.

Dr. Nair is still a visionary, and the fields are white unto harvest. If our missionary budget ever got to the place where only one missionary could be supported, G.S. Nair would be that missionary! I have never seen so much return on one's missionary dollar. It is a privilege to call this modern-day Paul 'my friend,' and I wholeheartedly encourage you to help ride the wave of what God is doing in India."

Dr. Jeff Amsbaugh, Pastor   **Greater Rhode Island**
Johnstown, RI   **Baptist Temple**

"Dr. Nair is a specially gifted man of vision for his people and the world. Taking biblical doctrinal stands has cost him potential support, but he remains committed to the Gospel and its proclamation. Compromise is not an option.

From the colleges, children's homes, layman's schools, church plants, I can enthusiastically commend the ministry of PBMI, and its founder, Dr. G.S. Nair.

Our church (of 70 members) supports the ministry with a minimum commitment of over $700 per month and then always tries to give additional funds as we are made aware of special needs."

Rev. Stuart G. Hunt, Pastor   **First Baptist Church**
Damascus, PA

A testimonial by Rev. Mathan K. Kurian
Academic Dean
Peoples Baptist Bible College and Seminary
Trivandrum, Kerala State, India

DR. G.S. NAIR — A LIVING LEGEND WITH A GIANT LIFE OF FAITH AND PRAYER.

It is indeed a great privilege to live during the time of a man of God like Dr. G.S. Nair, who is mightily used by God specially in a nation and generally around the globe. I have been literally amazed by his life and the way the Lord has been using him for His glory for the last forty plus years. I have had the privilege of serving the Lord with Dr. Nair for the past twenty-two years.

During this long period of time, Dr. Nair and the dedicated team with him has taught and trained and discipled more than 25,000 people including pastors, evangelists, and laymen through Bible colleges, extension schools, pastors' meetings, seminars, and special classes all over India, Nepal, and Myanmar.

A man of passion...

He has the ability to get the job done. His result-producing leadership is a part of his character. He always stands for what is right with backbone. He has a consistent conviction. His commitment, character, communication, competence, and courage, etc., cannot be compared easily. He has a real vision of mission and the passion and charisma to achieve it with a positive attitude and self-discipline by trusting the Lord. He is generous and listening. His discerning spirit and problem-solving ability are challenging. His administrative ability and leadership qualities are unique. Yes, he is a well-balanced, great, godly man.

A man of prayer and devotion...

Even though he's so busy, he finds time to read, meditate, and study the Word personally and teach others. And he finds time for personal private prayer every morning and evening and even other times, too. He motivates others to trust in the Lord for everything. He has an exemplary lifestyle that is completely controlled by the Word, prayer, and faith.

And a man of compassion...

He has a pastor's heart, and the churches he has established are evidence of it. The Bible colleges and the extension Bible schools he started across the nation prove his desire to give competent theological education to the people who will be able to teach others. Tailoring schools, technical institutions, and other job-oriented projects show his concern for the unemployed. Children's homes, old age homes, a widows' care project, drug and leprosy rehabilitation centers, etc., are evidences of his compassionate heart.

The world is yet to see what the Lord is going to do in and through him in the days ahead. It is my sincere wish and prayer that the Lord may keep on using him more effectively until the Master's return.

Truly he is a man of prayer, faith, courage, conviction, vision, passion, compassion, and much more ... I would say, *A LIVING LEGEND*..., "holding forth the word of life; that he may rejoice in the day of Christ, that he had not run in vain, neither labored in vain."

G.S. NAIR BIOGRAPHY

Dr. G.S. Nair is a Baptist pastor and evangelist from Trivandrum, Kerala State, India. As a Hindu high caste Army man, he was a harsh and outspoken critic of Christianity until he was converted while recuperating from tuberculosis at a Baptist Mid-Missions Hospital in 1972.

He pastors Peoples Baptist Church in Trivandrum. In 1976 he founded and is president of Peoples Baptist Ministries to India (PBMI), which is the outreach ministry of Peoples Baptist Church Trivandrum, Kerala State, India.

Under Dr. Nair's leadership, PBMI has established more than 2,700 churches with over 250,000 members. It has built and now operates twenty orphanages, three Bible colleges, a seminary, eight Bible college extension schools, seven private Christian schools, a ministry to lepers, a home for abused girls, and more, all in India, Nepal, and Burma.

Nair earned a Bachelor of Religious Education (B.R.E.) and Bachelor of Theology (B.Th.) from Berean Baptist Bible College and Seminary in Bangalore, India.

He was honored with Doctor of Ministry (D.Min.) degrees from Maranatha Baptist University, Watertown, WI, and Maryland Baptist Bible College, Elkton, Maryland, in recognition of his life work in education.

Dr. Nair's quotes and favorite sayings

You don't have to look into the world for worldliness, you can see it in today's church.

The heart of every problem is the problem of the heart.

You can't take Christ out of the church, or if you do, there is no real church.

Christ should be the heart of your life.

When you have a problem, don't worry about the greatness of the problem, but relax in the greatness of God.

Disappointment can be turned to an appointment with God.

Your decision of spiritual matters must be based on the Word of God, not on your logical reasoning.

Your logic may lead you to a wrong direction. Consider Jonah.

Don't ever take any counsel from a backslider.

The Devil knows your weaker points better than you.

You should be a successful Christian, but your success is to glorify God.

Complacency is a deadly foe against Christian growth.

Our call is from Heaven to Heaven.

Our attitude toward the work determines whether God's name is slandered.

Satan must be recognized in all church conflicts.

Prayerless people are disobedient, and disobedient people do not pray.

We must trust the Lord—not our prayer effort.

It is possible to be religious without being a child of God.

There is no pillow so soft as a clear conscience.

I don't trust anybody because I don't trust myself.

Your background doesn't matter if God has called you for ministry.

Don't live upon past success but live by present strength upon the Lord.

Know Him so closely that you cannot separate from Him.

You are not required to be eloquent, brilliant, able, or successful but Faithful.

You cannot do the Lord's ministry in man's power.

God never shows you the entire plan He has for you at the beginning.

I strongly believe evangelism without discipleship doesn't work.

The curse of Third World Christianity is the outstretched hand.

God is no man's debtor.

If you're not growing, you're dying.

PBMI STATEMENT OF FAITH

✝ We believe that the Bible is the verbally inspired and infallible, authoritative Word of God—that it is our final authority in all matters of faith and practice. We believe that God has preserved his word for English speaking people, in the King James Bible (2 Tim. 3:16–17; 2 Pet. 1:20–21; Matt. 24:35).

✝ We believe there is one God eternally existent in three persons: Father, Son, and Holy Spirit (Deut. 6:4, 4:35; Matt. 3:16–17; Ps. 9:7; Jn. 10:30; Jn. 14:26; 1 Jn. 5:7).

✝ We believe in the Deity of Christ; His virgin birth; His shed blood for atonement of sin; His bodily resurrection; His ascension into Heaven, there to be our Intercessor; His Lordship over all creation (Jn. 1:1–3; 1 Jn. 1:7; Heb. 9:11, 12; 1 Pet. 1:18–19; 1 Cor. 15:3–4; Rom. 8:34; Heb. 7:25; Matt. 28:18, Phil. 2:9–11).

✝ We believe that the Holy Spirit convicts of sin, makes believers children of God through the new birth, assuring them of Heaven, and by His indwelling enables Christians to live a Godly life (Jn. 16:8–11; Titus 3:5; 1 Cor. 12:13; 1 Cor. 6:19–20; Rom. 8:14, 16; Rom. 8: 1–4; Gal. 5:16; Eph. 5:9, 18).

✝ We believe that all men are sinners by nature and choice, sinful and lost, and have within themselves no possible means of salvation without Christ (Rom. 3:10, 23; Rom. 5:12; Eph. 2:8–9; Eph. 2:1–3, 12; Titus 3:5).

✝ We believe in Salvation by grace through faith; that Salvation is the free gift of God, not by any virtue or works of man, but received only by personal faith in the Lord Jesus Christ; and that all true believers possess the gift of eternal life, a perfect righteousness, sonship in the family of God, and the divine guarantee that they shall never perish (Jn. 3:16; Eph. 2:8–9; Titus 3:5; Jn. 1:12; Jn. 10:28; Jn. 3:18).

✝ We believe in the existence of Satan the deceiver and god of this present world; that he was defeated and judged at the cross, and therefore his final doom is certain (Jn. 8:44; Job 1:6–12; Job 2:1–8; 2 Cor. 4:4; Eph. 2:2; 1 Jn. 3:8; 1 Jn. 5:18; 1 Jn. 4:4; Rev. 20:10).

† We believe in the second coming of Christ; the time being unrevealed but always imminent; that when He comes He will first by resurrection of the dead and the translation (rapture) of the living remove from the earth His waiting Church; then pour out the righteous judgements of God upon the unbelieving world, afterwards descend with His Church and establish His glorious and literal kingdom over all nations for a thousand years (Jn. 14:1–3; Acts 1:11; 1 Thess. 4:13–18; 1 Cor. 15:51–57; Rev. 6–9; Rev. 19:11–20:6).

† We believe that the spirits of the saved, at death, go immediately to be with Christ in Heaven; that at His second coming their works will be judged and rewards determined; that the spirits of the unsaved at death descend immediately into Hell until the final day of judgement, at which time their bodies shall be raised from the grave, judged, and cast into the lake of fire, the place of final and everlasting punishment (2 Cor. 5:6–10; Luke 16:19–31; Rev. 20:11–15).

† We believe in the priesthood of all believers, that Christ is our High Priest and through Him every born-again person has direct access into God's presence without the need of a human priest; that the believer has the right and responsibility to personally study and interpret the Scriptures, guided by the Holy Spirit (1 Pet. 2:9; 1 Tim. 2:5; Heb. 7:17–28; Heb. 6:20; Heb. 4:14–16; Jn. 14:26; Jn. 16:13; 2 Pet. 1:19–21; 1 Pet. 2:2; 2 Tim. 2:15).

† We believe that a local New Testament Church is an organized body of born-again baptized believers practicing the scriptural ordinances and actively engaged in fulfilling the Great Commission (Matt. 28:18–20; 1 Cor. 11:23–34).

† We believe the officers of the church are pastors and deacons. In Scripture the pastor is also referred to as an elder. The two terms describe the same office (1 Tim. 3:1–13; Phil. 1:4).

Organizational Chart

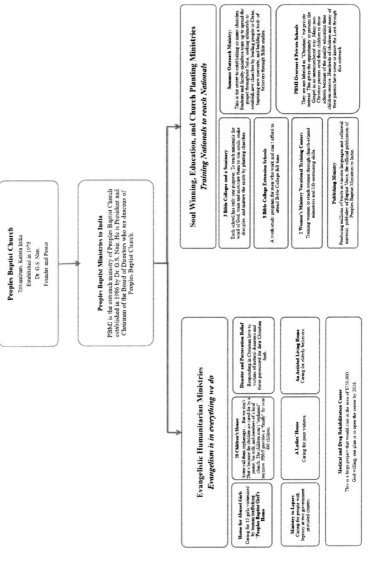

Peoples Baptist Church

Trivandrum, Kerala India

Established in 1978

Dr. G.S. Nair,

Founder and Pastor

Peoples Baptist Ministries to India

PBMI is the outreach ministry of Peoples Baptist Church established in 1986 by Dr. G.S. Nair. He is President and Chairman of the Board of Directors who are deacons of Peoples Baptist Church.

Soul Winning, Education, and Church Planting Ministries
Training Nationals to reach Nationals

3 Bible Colleges and a Seminary

Each school has only one purpose: To teach nationals the word of God, train and motivate them to win souls, make disciples, and mature the saints by planting churches.

5 Bible College Extension Schools

A work-study program for men who work and can't afford to attend Bible College full time.

2 Women's Ministry Vocational Training Centers

Training women to reach women through church-related ministries and life-sustaining skills.

Publishing Ministry

Producing millions of tracts in various languages and colloateral material; publisher of *Reign Voice*, the official publication of Peoples Baptist Ministries to India

Summer Outreach Ministry:

This is the secret to establishing so many churches. Students and faculty members team up to spread the gospel throughout India, seeking ultimately to establish new churches by leading people to Christ, baptizing new converts, and building a body of believers through Bible studies.

PBMI Overseas 6 Private Schools

They are not labeled as "Christian," but private instead. This gives the opportunity to present the Gospel in an unencumbered way. Many non-Christian parents send their children to these schools because of the quality education their children receive. Hundreds of children and many of their parents have come to know the Lord through this outreach.

Evangelistic Humanitarian Ministries
Evangelism is in everything we do

Home for Abused Girls

Caring for 15 girls victimized by human trafficking, "Peoples Baptist Girl's Home

20 Children's Home

Some call them orphanages... But we don't. That's because the children are cared for by a pastor, his wife, and members of a local church. The children aren't "orphaned" anymore. PBMI provides a "family" for over 400 children.

Disaster and Persecution Relief

Responding in Christian love to victims of natural disasters and those persecuted for their Christian faith.

An Assisted Living Home

Caring for elderly believers.

Ministry to Lepers

Caring for people with leprosy at two government provided centers.

A Ladies' Home

Caring for poor widows.

Medical and Drug Rehabilitation Center

This is a large project that would cost in the area of $750,000. God willing, our plan is to open the center by 2018.

ABOUT THE AUTHOR

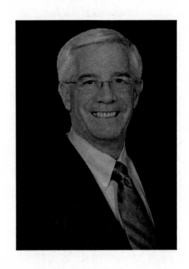

JACK MCELROY is an entrepreneur, businessman, publisher, and author.

He has authored:

> *How I Lost My Fear of Death and How You Can Too*

> *Which Bible Would Jesus Use?—The Bible Version Controversy Explained and Resolved*

> *Jenna's Cure: How an American dad discovered a European cure for his desperately ill daughter's autoimmune disease* (forthcoming)

He is co-author of:

> *Adoniram Judson's Soul Winning Secrets Revealed: An Inspiring Look at the Tools Used by "Jesus Christ's Man" in Burma.*

> *Can You Trust Just One Bible?*

Jack was raised as a Roman Catholic—attending a Catholic grammar and Jesuit high school. His life changed in 1978 when he became a Born Again Christian after a 2-year search for the answer to the question: "What happens to you **after** you die?"

He has been the president of McElroy Electronics Corporation for over 35 years.

He co-founded and was president of Dutchess County Cellular Telephone Corporation in Poughkeepsie, NY; co-founded and was chief manager of Minneapolis Cellular Telephone Company, LLC, in Minneapolis, MN; and co-founded and is president of McElroy Publishing and McElroy Rare Bible Page Collections.

He has taught Bible doctrine to all age groups, from preschoolers to adults. He served as a youth leader for over 20 years and as a deacon at a Baptist church for over 12 years. He loves the word of God and is reading through the King James Bible for the 20th time.

Although he is a member of a Baptist church, Jack describes his "religion" as a "Born Again Bible Believer."

He holds a Bachelor of Science degree in Industrial Management from Lowell Technological Institute (now UMass Lowell). Jack and Susan have been happily married for 40 years. They have four children and three grandchildren.

Visit his website at **http://jackmcelroy.com/**

Other Books by the Author

Adoniram Judson's Soul Winning Secrets Revealed—An Inspiring Look at the Tools Used by "Jesus Christ's Man" in Burma, Co-authored with Daw Tin Tin Aye

Adoniram Judson, Jr. (1788–1850) said, "The motto of every missionary, whether preacher, printer, or schoolmaster, ought to be 'Devoted for life.'" Now for the first time, you can read and study the arsenal of "soul winning tools" used by "The Father of American Foreign Missions." This is the only book in the world that contains an outstanding collection of the four most prominent tracts Judson used as well as the first translation of Judson's newly discovered fifth tract that he used as a primer on the Old Testament promises of a Savior.

How I Lost My Fear of Death and How You Can Too is a unique and universal soul winning book you can give to anybody of any religion without fear of insulting them. It's perfect for folks who need more detailed information before committing their lives to Christ. It cuts to the chase, focusing on what ten major religions say about what you must **DO** to get eternal life versus what

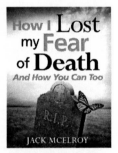

Christ has already **DONE**. Over 110 Scripture references and 50 pictures and illustrations present the Gospel to readers from ages 12 and up; Compact and convenient 5"× 7" size; 168 easy-to-read pages.

WHICH BIBLE WOULD JESUS USE?
The Bible Version Controversy Explained and Resolved

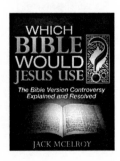

By answering the simple question, "If Jesus came to your church, which Bible would he use?" the Bible version controversy is settled once and for all. This book convincingly explains why the Lord can't use the NIV, ESV, NASB, NLT, NRSV, or any modern version including the New King James Version without looking foolish and destroying the brand he's established for the past 400 years. His choice is proven to be the King James Bible.

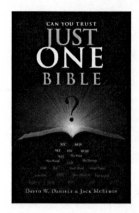

Can You Trust Just One Bible? Co-authored with David W. Daniels of Chick Publications.

In early 2015, authors Jack McElroy and David W. Daniels felt a burden to help other Christians whose faith was being challenged. They recorded two unrehearsed interviews where they answered many anti-KJV accusations to show you WHY you CAN trust just one Bible—The King James Version. The videos are available on YouTube; however, this printed book edition has much MORE information and documentation. This easy-to-read book will give you the tools, insights, and revelations to help you to convince others (and yourself) that we hold in our hands the very words of the living God in English, in the King James Bible.

Other Titles from McElroy Publishing include:

How to Be a Successful Camp Counselor

Mastering Leadership in the Christian Camp and Related Ministries

How to Be a Great Camp Counselor

The Camp Counselor's Handbook of over 90 Games and Activities Just for Rainy Days!

The Complete Encyclopedia of Christian Camp Directing and Programming

CPSIA information can be obtained
at www.ICGtesting.com
Printed in the USA
FSOW01n1414150217
30683FS